MUHAMMAD ALI

THE GREATEST OF ALL TIME

ROBERT CASSIDY

PUBLICATIONS INTERNATIONAL, LTD.

Robert Cassidy is the co-author of the book *Boxing Legends of All Time*. He is a contributing writer for *The Ring, KO, World Boxing,* and the *British Boxing News*. He has written about boxing for numerous publications, including *Newsday*, the *New York Post*, and the *Los Angeles Times*.

Editorial Assistance: Edward Maloney

ACKNOWLEDGMENTS:
Publications International, Ltd., has made every effort to locate the owners of all copyrighted material to obtain permission to use the selections that appear in this book. Any errors or omissions are unintentional; corrections, if necessary, will be made in future editions.

Pages 32, 59, 108–109, 134–135, 136, and 145: Quotes reprinted with the permission of Simon & Schuster from *Muhammad Ali: His Life and Times* by Thomas Hauser. Copyright © 1991 by Thomas Hauser and Muhammad Ali.

Photo credits:
Front cover: **AP/Wide World Photos** (background); **Michael Cooper/Allsport USA** (right).

AP/Wide World Photos: 6, 10, 20, 28, 37, 38, 47, 48, 51, 60, 68, 75, 81, 90, 91, 100, 113, 118, 129, 136, 153; **Allsport USA:** Hulton Deutsch: 33; MSI: 117; **Archive Photos:** 17, 23, 43; Neal Boenzi/New York Times Co.: 59; Express Newspapers: 122; Faleh Keibar/Reuters: 147; **FPG International:** 18; Alan-Michael Braveman: 82; **Globe Photos, Inc.:** 9, 52, 56, 108; John Barrett: 157; Neil Leifer: 72; Lisa Rose: 150; Hy Simon: 154; **Sports Illustrated © Time Inc.:** 126; James Drake: 132; John Iacono: 139, 140; Peter Read Miller: 148; Tony Triolo: 85, 95; **UPI/Corbis-Bettmann:** 103.

Contents

Chapter 1: The Early Rounds 4

Chapter 2: Olympic Gold 13

Chapter 3: Rewriting the Rules 21

Chapter 4: "The Big, Ugly Bear" 34

Chapter 5: Child of the '60s 45

Chapter 6: Exile 55

Chapter 7: The Fight of the Century 65

Chapter 8: The Road Back 78

Chapter 9: The Rumble in the Jungle 87

Chapter 10: The Thrilla in Manila 97

Chapter 11: Jabbing with Cosell 107

Chapter 12: The World's Champion 114

Chapter 13: The Spinks Jinx 124

Chapter 14: The Roar of the Crowd 134

Chapter 15: The Legend Lives On 144

Chapter 16: Ali's Legacy 155

Appendix: Ali's Professional Record 159

The Early Rounds

Cassius Clay first entered the ring at age 12. Soon, the kid with the quick hands and fast mouth proclaimed himself the next heavyweight champion of the world.

I f not for the actions of a petty thief, the world may have never been introduced to one of the most recognizable athletes to walk the face of this earth. If not for a young boy's anguish over a stolen bicycle, the greatest heavyweight champion in the history of boxing may have never been compelled to pursue his sport.

That champion is Muhammad Ali.

Ali was born Cassius Marcellus Clay Jr. on January 17, 1942, in Louisville, Kentucky. In 1954, when he was 12 years old, Clay and a friend rode their bicycles to the Columbia Auditorium, where local merchants were selling their goods at a neighborhood bazaar. They remained at the bazaar for much of the day, and when it was time to go home Clay discovered that his bike had been stolen. The future heavyweight champion of the world was visibly upset, and some adults at the bazaar directed him to a police officer in the basement. Clay ventured down the stairs to report the crime and discovered officer Joe Martin teaching young boys how to box. The young Clay told the officer that he would someday beat up the boy who stole his bike. Martin suggested that he should learn how to fight first. At that moment in time, Cassius Clay had found his calling.

The Clay family lived on Grand Avenue in a middle-class neighborhood on the west end of Louisville that was predominantly made up of African Americans. His father, Cassius Marcellus Clay Sr., worked as a sign painter, and his mother, Odessa Grady Clay, worked as a household domestic. Young Cassius Clay and his brother, Rudy, avoided trouble while growing up, and when they reached their teens they often accompanied their father on painting jobs. On June 11, 1960, Cassius graduated from Central High School.

But long before that, Clay began to earn his degree in the sweet science. Shortly after his bike was stolen, Clay joined the Columbia Gym as a member of Martin's amateur boxing team. Jimmy Ellis, who in 1968 would win the WBA heavyweight title during Clay's exile from boxing, also trained at the same gym, and the two became lifelong friends. After spending just six weeks training with Martin, the 89-pound Clay fought his first amateur fight and won a split decision over another novice, Ronnie O'Keefe. Thus began his love affair with boxing.

Although Clay did not immediately distinguish himself as a future champ, his skills began to blossom a year later. Martin has said that young Cassius had

Cassius, with his brother, Rudy (left), *in 1960. One of Clay's unorthodox methods to sharpen his reflexes was to dodge rocks thrown by his brother.*

more determination than most of the fighters his age and that his tremendous hand and foot speed were the first signs of future success. As a teenager, Clay was obsessed with boxing, and his passion for the sport was demonstrated by the amount of time he devoted to improving. To help sharpen his reflexes, Clay would tell his younger brother to throw rocks at him. And no matter how many rocks Rudy threw at him, Cassius managed to dodge each rock. Martin would later call him the hardest working kid he ever met.

Even as an amateur fighter, there was an aura about Clay. His speed and reflexes were clearly an asset during amateur competitions, and it was evident early on that Clay's success would hinge on his quick left jab. His flashy style, often criticized by boxing trainers, became a trademark that he would carry throughout his entire pro career.

"He moved a lot, which was the style I favored," said Vic Zimet, a veteran amateur boxing official who would later work against Clay. "He was very stylish even as a young fighter. It was the style of the 1930s, reminiscent of the great boxer Benny Leonard. That's how I taught my boxers how to box."

Also obvious from his amateur days was Clay's effusive personality. He was extremely outgoing, confident, and talkative.

"The first thing that entered his brain rolled right off his tongue."
–Historian Hank Kaplan, on Clay

"I've known Muhammad a long time, and he was always a lot of fun," said Hank Kaplan, the Miami-based boxing historian. "The first thing that entered his brain rolled right off his tongue. Some people would use discretion before they spoke, think about what they were saying. Not Muhammad. He was always honest. He's been that way since he was a kid."

If the world at large knew very little about Cassius Clay, the slick-fighting light heavyweight from Louisville took it upon himself to change that. In February 1957, Angelo Dundee, Clay's future trainer, was in Louisville, where Willie Pastrano was scheduled to fight a 10-round bout against John Holman. (Pastrano was also trained by Dundee, and in 1963 he would win the world light-heavyweight title.) Clay, who was 15 at the time, called Dundee on the phone and invited himself up to Pastrano's room. When he arrived there, he spent the evening talking boxing and told both Dundee and Pastrano that he would one day become heavyweight champion of the world.

But Clay's outward confidence and fearless forecasts of fame were not popular within the conservative amateur boxing establishment. In the ring and out, Clay was clearly cut from a different mold. Even as a teenager, he understood the value of media exposure, and he became a relentless self-promoter. At one amateur tournament, he even handed out glossy pictures of himself. However, this was an era in which the heroes of the ring—heavyweight champions like Joe Louis, Rocky Marciano, and Floyd Patterson—were humble and dignified men. The world was not yet ready for an athlete who drew constant attention to himself. Initially, his opponents, and even his teammates, thought he was more style than substance. The feeling was that a fighter who clamored for the spotlight had to be diverting attention from some hidden weakness.

"At first, he was just a bigmouth with a lot of speed," said Sean Curtin, who competed in an amateur tournament with Clay in 1958 and remains active in boxing today as a pro referee. "He was very cocky, and

Boxing historians agree that no heavyweight in history could approach the young Clay (right) in terms of natural speed, reflexes, and athleticism.

nobody liked that about him. But he had so much talent. I really started to appreciate him when he beat Allen Hudson, who won the Pan Am Games as a heavyweight. It was a tough fight and Clay was really a light heavyweight."

Nikos and Petros Spanakos, a pair of fighting twins out of New York City, ascended the ranks of amateur boxing with Clay. They boxed together in numerous national and international competitions. Their first encounter with him came in 1959 at the Pan Am Games trials in Madison, Wisconsin.

"I first saw him at the weigh-in during the Pan Am trials," recalled Petros. "He was punching the heavy bag and shadowboxing. At the weigh-in, the boxers are usually quiet and dignified. But Cassius was try-

New York Golden Gloves champion Tony Madigan, who hailed from Australia, lost a close decision to Clay in this 1959 intercity bout.

ing to get all the attention at the weigh-in. He was running around from photographer to photographer trying to get his picture in the paper. I just wrote him off as a young, crazy kid."

Nikos Spanakos, who was Clay's teammate on the 1960 U.S. Olympic boxing team, had a similar recollection of his first experience around the future heavyweight champion of the world. "The first time we saw him, he was this brash, young teenager with a big mouth," he said. "Cassius always demanded attention. That made him unpopular with other fighters. He was always talking, always shadowboxing in your face. Usually, guys like that put up a facade because they can't fight. But he could fight. I give him credit: When the going got tough, he hung in there."

The only times Nikos could recall Clay in a state of introspective silence were the moments before he entered the ring. "He'd get down on his knees and pray very fervently before each fight," recalled Nikos. "He was a Christian then, and he took religion very seriously."

Clay began to earn the respect of his peers by outshining them. When the bell rang, his words were replaced by actions. His hand speed and lightning left jab were often too much for his opponents to overcome. And if he appeared out of control outside the ring, he was in complete control inside it.

Dundee learned as much the second time he met the young boxer. Dundee and Pastrano had returned to Louisville in 1959. This time Pastrano, now ranked among the top light heavyweights in the world, was there to fight Alonzo Johnson. Clay asked Dundee if he could spar with Pastrano. Although Clay was just 17, he outboxed Pastrano for one round before the trainer halted the session. "He was so quick and agile," recalled Dundee. "Willie couldn't do nothing with him."

If the ostentatious Clay was slow to win the respect of his peers and coaches, there was one aspect of his approach to boxing that no one could criticize. It was his dire commitment to training. He did not drink or smoke and eschewed unhealthy food prior to fights.

"When it came to training, he was the first one at the track and the last one to leave," said Petros Spanakos. "The same thing at the gym. He'd be there an hour before everyone else and leave an hour after everyone else. He loved to train. He was the most focused person I ever met. He was a guy who was focused at the age of 12. At that age, he devoted his whole life to boxing."

By the time Clay was 18 years old, he had won two National Golden Gloves crowns and two National AAU titles. Yet, while Olympic glory beckoned, there were still those who remained unconvinced that the "Louisville Lip" could back up his lofty boasts.

"From the first time I saw him, he was telling everyone he was going to win a gold medal and then the heavyweight championship of the world," said Petros Spanakos. "We did a lot of traveling with the national team, and once in a while some of the guys would look around the room and pick who they thought would go on and win a world championship. No one ever picked Cassius."

CHAPTER 2

Olympic Gold

Overcoming a fear of flying, Clay traveled to Rome for the 1960 Olympics. He dazzled and dazed his three light-heavyweight foes to claim the gold medal.

There wasn't anything that 18-year-old Cassius Clay feared inside a boxing ring. However, his fear of flying nearly prevented him from going to the 1960 Olympics in Rome.

Clay had endured a rough flight on the way to the U.S. Olympic trials in California. After winning the tournament, and earning a spot on the team, Clay told his coach, Joe Martin, that he would not fly to Rome to participate in the Summer Games.

It was shocking news to Martin. Clay regularly boasted that he would one day win an Olympic gold medal and then the heavyweight title. Suddenly, he had refused to fly and was willing to pass up the opportunity of a lifetime. Clay wanted to travel by boat, but he was told that he had to fly with the rest of the boxing team. Finally, Martin convinced him to fly to Rome, telling the young fighter that winning a gold medal would be a very important first step toward a lifetime of fantastic achievements.

"He was terrified of flying," said Nikos Spanakos, the Brooklyn featherweight who was Clay's teammate on the U.S. Olympic team. "There were times when he was an amateur that he'd take a train across the country to get to a tournament. When we were flying over to Rome, the coach gave each of us a sleeping pill. When Cassius woke up, he started acting out. I said, 'Coach, give him another pill.'"

> **"[Clay] was terrified of flying. There were times when he was an amateur that he'd take a train across the country to get to a tournament."**
> **—Olympic teammate Nikos Spanakos**

However, once Clay arrived in Rome, he felt completely at ease.

"The whole boxing team just stayed in and rested," said Spanakos. "We didn't march in the parade and we didn't go to the audience with the Pope. A lot of us were antisocial, if that's the proper way to put it. But not Cassius."

The Louisville fighter maximized his Olympic experience by introducing himself to athletes from all over the world. His outgoing personality and natural gift of gab allowed him to befriend many in the Olympic Village. He took pictures with numerous athletes and exchanged Olympic patches and souvenirs with people from all over the globe.

"Whenever he could gather attention, he would do it," said Spanakos. "He was very outgoing. He became the darling of the Olympics strictly on his personality."

The 1960 Olympics boasted an array of world-class athletes, and clearly Cassius Clay was one of them. Ultimately, Clay would dwarf all the other participants of the '60 Games in terms of popularity and fame. But at the time, he was merely a sidebar to many larger stories that were unfolding in Rome.

Wilma Rudolph, a 20-year-old sprinter from Tennessee who had walked with a brace on her left leg as a child, became the first U.S. woman to capture three gold medals; she won the 100 and 200 meters and ran the anchor leg of the winning 4×100 relay team. Ethiopia's Abebe Bikila shocked the world when he won a gold medal in the marathon, completing the entire 26-mile race in his bare feet. Al Oerter, of the U.S., won the second of his Olympic-record four gold medals in the discus.

The United States sent a Dream Team of sorts to participate in the basketball competition. The U.S. went 8–0 in the tournament and captured the gold medal. The team had 10 members who would later play in the NBA, including Hall of Famers Jerry West, Oscar Robertson, Walt Bellamy, and Jerry Lucas.

The boxing venue at the 1960 Olympic Games was also brimming with potential. Clay's reputation had been solidified with a string of successful victories back in the United States, and expectations for him were high in Rome. He was favored to bring home a gold medal in the 178-pound division. Another favorite to win gold was two-time AAU champion Wilbert "Skeeter" McClure, of Toledo, Ohio.

The competition also included some other notable fighters. Future two-division champion and Hall of Famer Nino Benvenuti, of Italy, won a gold medal in the welterweight division. Two other Italian fighters, Carmelo Bossi and Sandro Lopopolo, captured silver medals and would later become professional world champions. Ghana's Clement Quartey became the first black African to win a boxing medal when he won a silver in the junior-welterweight division. Thirty-four years later, his son, Ike Quartey, would become the WBA welterweight champion.

Clay's first Olympic bout came against Belgium's Yvon Becaus, and Clay scored a second-round knock-out. Next came the Soviet Union's Guennadiy Chatkov, who had won a gold medal in the middleweight division at the 1956 Olympics. Clay handled Chatkov easily, scoring a unanimous 5–0 decision.

In the semifinals, Clay was matched with a familiar rival, Anthony Madigan. Although Madigan represented Australia, he had trained in New York and had won a Golden Gloves title in 1959. He and Clay had fought in Chicago's Tournament of Champions. Clay won the rousing contest, and it was that fight that marked the beginning of his rise to national stardom. When they met again at the Olympics, Madigan fought determinedly but was decisively outpointed, as Clay earned another 5–0 decision.

"I was impressed with [Clay's] ability, but I always wondered about his heart," said Spanakos. "But the kid could fight. He had some tough fights in Rome. The Madigan fight was a war. Whenever Cassius was in a tough fight, he'd rise to the occasion."

Clay again defeated Tony Madigan, this time fighting for Australia, in the semifinal bout at the 1960 Olympics.

Clay would have to rise to the occasion one more time. In the finals, his opponent was Poland's Zbigniew Pietrzykowski, who had competed in the 1956 Olympics but lost in a first-round fight. Still, the 28-year-old Pietrzykowski's credentials were impressive. He was a veteran of over 200 fights and was a three-time European amateur champion.

As the gold-medal bout began, Clay showed more style than substance. He danced swiftly away from his southpaw opponent and did little in the way of scoring any points. Clay took a few more chances offensively in the second round, but heading into the final round most observers felt the fight was even. That's when Clay took control.

Clay's speed overwhelmed Pietrzykowski in the third round. The Louisville teenager boxed brilliantly and stunned his mature opponent with swift combinations. At the final bell, Pietrzykowski was bloodied and dazed. When it was over, Clay was awarded a 5–0 unanimous decision and the gold medal.

Two of Clay's teammates, Edward Crook (middleweight) and McClure (light middleweight), also brought home gold medals. McClure, who would go on to become a Top 10 pro middleweight, beat local favorite Bossi in a 3–0–2 decision for his gold.

Clay's victory was the first step toward his becoming just the second member of a very prestigious boxing fraternity. At the time, Floyd Patterson, who had won a gold medal in 1952, was the only American boxer to win an Olympic gold medal and the world heavyweight title. Clay would achieve that feat in 1964 by dethroning world champ Sonny Liston. In addition to Patterson and Clay, the club includes Joe Frazier, George Foreman, Leon Spinks, and Michael Spinks. Other U.S. medalists have also won the heavy-

Clay, flanked by teammates and gold medalists Eddie Crook (left) and Skeeter McClure, in Rome. Only Clay would enjoy great success as a pro.

weight crown: John Tate (bronze, 1976), Evander Holyfield (bronze, 1984), and Riddick Bowe (silver, 1988).

After winning the medal, Clay demonstrated that at the age of 18 he already had a way of handling the media. In *Muhammad Ali: His Life and Times,* author Thomas Hauser recounted an exchange between Clay and a reporter from the Soviet Union. The reporter asked how it felt to earn an Olympic championship for the United States while there were still restaurants back home that refused to serve him because of the color of his skin.

"Tell your readers we got qualified people working on that problem and I'm not worried about the outcome," said Clay. "To me, the USA is the best country in the world, including yours."

Much has been written about what has happened to Clay's gold medal. While the fate of the medal itself is unclear, one thing is for certain: He cherished it. Clay regularly wore his gold medal in the Olympic Village and wore it often in the first few months after he returned home from Rome. One story that has turned into lore suggests that Clay threw the medal into the Ohio River after he was refused service at a whites-only restaurant and chased out of the dining hall by members of a motorcycle gang. However, a 1992 *Sports Illustrated* story quotes Hauser, arguably the foremost authority on Muhammad Ali, as saying that he simply lost the medal.

At the 1996 Olympic Games in Atlanta, Ali lit the torch at the opening ceremony. Later, during a stirring ceremony, he was presented with another gold medal to replace the one that was lost.

Back in 1960, Clay was treated to a hero's welcome when he returned home to Louisville after his Olympic

Unlike many boxers, Cassius, seen here with his brother and parents on his return from Rome, always had the support of his family.

triumph. A 25-car parade, led by police cars with their sirens blaring, escorted the champion home. Cassius Clay was Louisville's biggest boxing hero since Marvin Hart, who knocked out Jack Root to win the heavyweight title in 1905.

While in Rome, Clay had forged a friendship with Wilma Rudolph, who visited the fighter a few months after the Olympics. Clay chauffeured Rudolph around town in his pink Cadillac convertible, shouting to passersby: "I am the greatest.... This is Wilma Rudolph; she's the greatest."

"I saw him at the very beginning," recalled Rudolph in *Sports Illustrated.* "It was bedlam. I always told him, 'You should be on stage.'"

It wasn't long before the world became Cassius Clay's stage.

CHAPTER 3

Rewriting the Rules

*From 1960 to 1963, Clay compiled a
perfect 19–0 record. The brash up-and-comer
predicted—often correctly—the round in
which his opponent would fall.*

W hen Cassius Clay returned from the Rome
Olympics, he was ready to turn the boxing
world upside down. There was never really
a question of whether he had the talent to accomplish
his lofty dreams. The more perplexing question was
whether the boxing world was ready for Cassius Clay.

Clay launched his pro career in an era when fighters did not write poems about their opponents. They
fought and they fought hard. Boxing was a lunch-pail
sport, and this brash Olympic champion seemed as
out of place as a Yuppie prancing through a construction site. Clay was like a kid in a toy store, only
his toy store was the sport of boxing.

While some of the game's grizzled veterans would
not immediately accept his boisterous personality, he

was clearly a breath of fresh air in a sport that had become stale. The Golden Age of boxing—when fights were a network TV staple and boxing clubs thrived in major cities—was coming to an end. But the boxer known as the "Louisville Lip" was clearly resuscitating his sport.

On October 29, 1960, the 18-year-old Clay made his professional debut at Freedom Hall in his hometown of Louisville, Kentucky. The opponent was Tunney Hunsaker, a part-time heavyweight who was the chief of police in Fayetteville, West Virginia, when he wasn't boxing. Although Hunsaker came into the ring with a 17–8 record, Clay won by a unanimous decision in six rounds.

Clay's enthusiasm for attracting attention to himself and his fights forever revolutionized the way boxing would be promoted. However, it wasn't enough for him to provide the sport with a new sales pitch; he was simultaneously revolutionizing the art of boxing itself. The sweet science was an art form to Clay. He combined grace, speed, agility, and power, and the result was a heavyweight who had the hand speed and reflexes of a welterweight.

There is an old adage in sports that says, "Speed covers a multitude of sins." The incredible speed that Clay possessed afforded him the luxury of committing some of boxing's cardinal sins. He often fought while carrying his hands at his waist, ignoring the textbook mandate that ordered fighters to carry their hands cheek high in order to block or parry punches. Clay's defense was his sharp reflexes and nimble legs, which often carried him away from danger. When stationary, he did not usually slip or duck punches; instead, he quickly pulled his head back, allowing incoming blows to fall harmlessly short. This technique is often frowned upon because the act of pulling back from punches leaves the practitioner's head in the direct line of fire for a follow-up punch.

"I remember Sarge Johnson, who coached the great 1976 U.S. Olympic team, used to tell his fighters, 'I don't want you to watch Ali; he does too many things wrong,'" said Vic Zimet, a veteran boxing trainer. "I'm a boxing purist. But if something works for you, what's wrong with it? Ali prided himself on his reflexes and his quickness. That's how he avoided trouble in the ring."

Clay continued to ignore his detractors. He was having too much fun rewriting the boxing rule book his own way.

In Clay's corner for his pro debut was trainer Fred Stoner. But the Louisville Sponsoring Group, a collection of 11 Louisville businessmen who financed the early part of Clay's career, thought they should find a

The Beatles (left to right: Paul McCartney, John Lennon, Ringo Starr, George Harrison) and Clay began their journeys as international and lifelong celebrities in February 1964.

more experienced trainer to handle their investment. The first option was legendary light-heavyweight champion Archie Moore. While Clay spent some time in Moore's training facility, the two fighters could not bridge the generation gap that separated them.

The next selection was trainer Angelo Dundee, who ran the Fifth Street Gym in Miami Beach, Florida. With Dundee in his corner, Clay knocked out Herb Siler in the fourth round of his second pro fight, and a partnership was formed that would last until the end of Clay's career.

Dundee had learned the game of boxing by observing the great trainers at Stillman's Gym in New York City. Among his tutors were Ray Arcel, Charlie Goldman, and Chickie Ferrara. Pairing an old-school trainer like Dundee with Clay hardly seemed like a formula for success. But Dundee's gentle demeanor and sly sense of humor made it the perfect match.

"I trained Muhammad in a different way," said Dundee. "I couldn't train him by the numbers. It was a completely different story with Muhammad. Boxing is a sport of individuals, and he was an individual. He had to be the innovator. I never made him feel like he was taking orders. I'd say to him, 'That was perfect the way you threw that left hook. You had your shoulder into it and you pivoted on your toe. It was perfect.' And even if he didn't throw it that way at that moment, he'd throw that way the next time he did it."

In a four-week span in 1961—from January 17 to February 21—Clay registered stoppages against Tony Esperti (KO 3), Jim Robinson (KO 1), and Donnie Fleeman (KO 7). Each bout took place in Miami Beach, which quickly became Clay's new headquarters. And at the center of it all was the Fifth Street Gym.

"The Fifth Street Gym in Miami had the same pull and mystique as Stillman's," said Dundee. "It was Stillman's at its southern-most point. Plenty of great fighters trained there, and Muhammad was always watching, always learning. He was a great student of styles. He could imitate any style."

The Fifth Street Gym was opened by Angelo's brother, Chris Dundee, in 1951, and it remained one of boxing's premier training facilities until it was torn down in 1993. Legendary fighters such as Sugar Ray Robinson, Jake LaMotta, Willie Pep, Kid Gavilan, and Sonny Liston trained there during stops in Florida.

When Clay arrived at the gym in 1960, Dundee had a fine stable of fighters training there on a daily basis. Among them were welterweight champion Luis Rodriguez and future light-heavyweight king Willie Pastrano. In Rodriguez and Pastrano, Clay found a pair of perfect role models.

"Rodriguez was very fond of Muhammad and vice versa," said Miami-based boxing historian Hank Kaplan. "Once Rodriguez saw him enter the gym, he'd yell out, *'Boca Grande,'* which was "Big Mouth" in Spanish. They joked a lot, but they had a mutual respect for each other."

Both Rodriguez and Pastrano had outstanding balance and footwork. Pastrano was as slick and elusive as any of his contemporaries, while Rodriguez was more of a boxer/puncher. Watching them work on a daily basis had an important impact on Clay's style. He routinely sparred with Pastrano and, although Rodriguez was only a welterweight, occasionally sparred with Rodriguez as well.

It hardly mattered that Clay was still developing his style and paying his dues as a preliminary fighter. He was anxious to take on the best heavyweights in the world.

"One day I came walking into the gym, and Muhammad was in the ring shadowboxing," recalled Kaplan, who worked as a publicist for some of Clay's early fights. "He looked over to me and said, 'Hank, who is the No. 10-ranked heavyweight in the world?' I said that I wasn't sure but that I would check for him. So he said, 'Well, find out because I want him.' This kid wanted to fight the 10th-best heavyweight in the world and he only had five fights as a pro."

Clay continued his impressive performances by beating Lamar Clark (KO 2), Duke Sabedong (W 10), and Alonzo Johnson (W 10). It was before the Sabedong fight, in Las Vegas, that he encountered another influence on his life. He appeared on a radio show with wrestler Gorgeous George and was impressed with the flair and braggadocio George used to hype his upcoming match. So, once again, Clay would borrow a little bit from another showman and incorporate it into his act.

Meanwhile, the time had come for Clay to meet his first ranked heavyweight. The opponent was Alex Miteff, and the fight took place in Freedom Hall on October 7, 1961. Miteff, an Argentine amateur champion, had an impressive pro résumé. He had beaten Wayne Bethea, drew with George Chuvalo, and lost decisions to Zora Folley and Eddie Machen. Miteff had been a top-10 heavyweight since 1957. Equipped with a potent body attack, he was clearly the best opponent Clay had faced.

"My manager didn't care much for me," said Miteff. "I fought everyone in their hometown, so I didn't think much about fighting Cassius Clay in Louisville.

I didn't know much about him at the time. He smiled a lot—that I remember. He was a very nice person."

Miteff was about to learn a lot more about Clay. Their fight was progressing at an even pace after five rounds, and Miteff hardly expected what happened next. The young heavyweight with a reputation for running caught him flush with a right hand and knocked him out in the sixth round.

"I don't remember the knockout," said Miteff. "What made him different from the other heavyweights that I fought was that he was very tall and very cool in the ring. He was a good boxer. He'd hit you, boom-boom-boom-boom, and he'd move around the ring. He did a lot of things wrong—or they were considered wrong back then. Because of that, I never thought he'd become a great success."

In the following fight, back at Freedom Hall on November 29, the world was introduced to a new phenomenon. Bursting with even more confidence after dispatching the rugged Miteff, Clay predicted he would knock out Willi Besmanoff in the seventh round. While he clearly could have won the fight sooner— and despite the protests of Dundee, who begged him to finish the job—Clay allowed Besmanoff to linger until the seventh round before knocking him out.

The 1962 campaign began with three straight four-round knockouts. The first to fall was Sonny Banks, who managed to drop Clay with a left hook in the first round before succumbing three rounds later. Don Warner (KO 4) and George Logan (KO 4) followed, and then it was time for another test. This time it would be against Billy Daniels, a former New York Golden Gloves champion. Daniels was a slick boxer who had compiled a 16–0 record as a pro. The fight

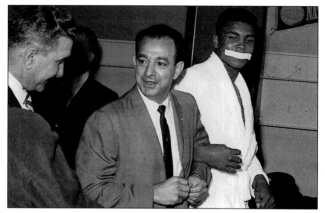

Unlike most trainers, Angelo Dundee (center) *thought that the best way to work with young Clay was to let the fighter be himself.*

took place on May 19, 1962, at St. Nicholas Arena in New York City.

"Most heavyweights at that time were plodders," said Vic Zimet, Daniels's trainer and co-manager. "Daniels was a good puncher with pretty good hand speed. And he could hurt you with a right hand."

The New York State Athletic Commission, as most commissions do, allowed a member of the opposing camp to witness the fighter's hands being wrapped. Zimet went to Clay's dressing room to watch Dundee wrap Cassius's hands. "When Clay noticed that I was there, he started reciting poetry about what he was going to do to Billy," recalled Zimet. "I figured I'd play my own head games, so I started whistling and ignoring him. Really, I just got a laugh out of it."

Again, Clay was confronted with a tough and talented opponent. The fight was close until Daniels began bleeding around the eyes. Daniels's ability to see Clay's punches diminished as the fight progressed, and it was finally stopped by referee Mark Conn in the seventh round.

"The referee and the doctor kept coming to the corner to check on Billy, but they were letting the fight go on," said Zimet. "Finally, in the seventh round, Mark Conn, who I knew when he was boxing, stopped the fight. I never protest when a referee stops a fight. It was a bad cut. But who knows what could have happened? It was a very close fight. People came up to me afterward and told me they thought Billy was winning."

After the Daniels fight, Clay brought his show west for a pair of fights in Los Angeles. The first was a fifth-round knockout of Alejandro Lavorante. He then closed out the 1962 campaign with a November 15 showdown against Archie Moore at the Memorial Sports Arena.

Moore was presented with the chance to teach his former pupil a lesson. A year earlier, Moore had been stripped of the light-heavyweight title by the New York State Athletic Commission for failing to meet the No. 1 contender. And while the fight with Clay would take place one month before his 49th birthday, Moore was still a capable contender. In '62 alone, he had already knocked out Lavorante in the 10th round and Howard King in one round and had fought to a 10-round draw with future light-heavyweight champ Pastrano.

Moore was a veteran of more than 200 pro fights and had scored well over 100 knockouts. Clay, who was 20, entered the ring with just 15 pro fights. At the time, there was no love lost between the combatants. Clay predicted a fourth-round knockout because of the rhyme: "Moore in Four." Moore said he had developed a new punch, called the "Lip Buttoner."

On this night, the student taught the teacher a painful lesson. Moore was dropped three times in the fourth round and the bout was stopped. Yes, Moore was gone by four. Clay opened 1963 with a third-round knockout of Charlie Powell, who once played in the National Football League and met such tough heavyweights as Floyd Patterson, Nino Valdes, and Charley Norkus. Clay's next opponent, New York's Doug Jones, would provide him with the stiffest test of his young career.

The stir for the Clay–Jones fight had reached a fever pitch in New York. The 26-year-old Jones had a 21–3–1 record and had knocked out the likes of Bobo Olson, Pete Rademacher, Bob Foster, and Zora Folley. Clay, now 17–0, had won nine straight by knockout and predicted that he would stop Jones in the fourth round. The fight took place on March 13, 1963, and it was so eagerly anticipated that, for the first time in its history, Madison Square Garden was sold out two days before an event.

Jones managed to wobble Clay with a stiff right hand in the opening seconds of the fight. After the fourth round had passed, and Clay had not scored a knockout, the Garden crowd turned against him. Jones seemed to have Clay stunned in Rounds 8 and 9, but the Louisville Lip remained composed. He boxed on his toes throughout the remainder of the contest and managed to secure a close unanimous decision. The scoring by rounds was 8–1–1 from the referee and 5–4–1 from the two judges.

"That was one of the worst decisions I was ever associated with," said Jones's manager, Rollie Hackmer. "Jones gave him a boxing lesson. Jones was countering his slapping jab. He'd catch the jab and counter with a right. Anybody that fought Clay had to be able to bob and weave and counterpunch. Jones was a master at both."

Although the controversial nature of the decision has made Jones a popular footnote to boxing history, the topic of that fight evokes bitterness from the former heavyweight contender.

"He never hurt me....A blind man could see who won that fight. There was no question about it: I won." —Doug Jones, who lost a disputed decision to Clay in 1963

"I never saw him fight before we fought and it didn't matter because I just look at a guy and know what I can do with him," Jones said in a 1996 interview in *The Ring* magazine. "I don't go into a fight with fear. I knew that Ali was big with his predictions. But I thought it was comical. I didn't think anyone could predict a round on me. His people thought Doug Jones was soft. They thought Ali would have another notch after this fight—a big notch."

When the decision was announced, the crowd at the Garden began to chant, "Fix! Fix!" While the outcome remains disputed, there was no disputing the bout's significance. In 1963, it was named Fight of the Year by *The Ring*.

"They say he was moving; I call it running," said Jones during the same interview. "The way I was moving, slipping, and sliding, I call that boxing. The man was constantly running. When you are running all the time, you shouldn't be in the fight game. His hands were fast, but they weren't fast enough to do anything to me. He never hurt me. I think maybe they bought the fight for him. A blind man could see who won that fight. There was no question about it: I won. But to know that he didn't make his prediction come true against me, that felt pretty good, too."

The lessons learned against fighters such as Daniels and Jones would serve Clay well in the future. However, it was the lessons learned by Dundee from the masters at Stillman's Gym that helped Clay overcome his next opponent, Henry Cooper.

Three months after the Jones fight, Clay traveled to London for a June 18 date against Cooper, who was the reigning British heavyweight champion. Clay predicted a fifth-round knockout, and from the outset it appeared he would have little trouble making good on his promise. Clay was too fast and his skills far superior to those possessed by his English counterpart. Cooper was bleeding badly from a cut above his left eye when, out of nowhere, he caught Clay with a left hook and dropped him in the waning moments of the fourth round. For the first time in his pro career, Clay was seriously hurt.

Dundee explained what happened next to author Thomas Hauser for the book *Muhammad Ali: His Life and Times:*

"[Muhammad] split his glove on the seam near the thumb. Actually, it happened in the first round. I spotted the tear then and told him, 'Keep your hand closed.' I didn't want anyone to see it because everything was going our way, if you know what I mean.

Although controversy surrounded their 1963 fight, Ali was equally as dominant in his March 1966 rematch with Englishman Henry Cooper.

Then, at the end of the fourth round, he got nailed... Cassius was hurt, no doubt about it...Then I helped the split a little, pulled it to the side, and made the referee aware there was a torn glove. I don't know how much time that got us. Maybe a minute, but it was enough. If we hadn't gotten the extra time, I don't know what would have happened."

When the fighting resumed, Clay emerged from the corner with a vengeance. He mercilessly battered Cooper for two minutes until the referee stopped the fight, keeping the prediction intact.

Clay was 21 years old and had a record of 19–0 with 15 knockouts. However, a "Big Ugly Bear" was looming on the horizon.

"The Big, Ugly Bear"

The 21-year-old Clay predicted an eighth-round knockout of Sonny Liston, the sullen, powerful champion. Both the title bout and the rematch would be clouded in controversy.

Cassius Clay believed he was destined to become heavyweight champion of the world. It was a conviction he shared with nearly everyone he came in contact with. As 1963 drew to a close, he was anxious to fulfill his date with destiny.

Many in the world of boxing doubted the pugilistic prophet from Louisville. Clay had certainly demonstrated talent and potential, but the seed of such doubt had been planted by the sheer power of Charles "Sonny" Liston.

Liston captured the heavyweight title with a stunning first-round knockout of Floyd Patterson. He was the antithesis of Clay. Liston did not recite poetry; he allowed his gloved fists to do all the talking. He was not chatty; he was sullen. He did not box with the grace and skill of Clay; he hunted his opponents in the ring and dispatched them without remorse or hesitation.

Clay's recent performances hardly convinced anyone that he was ready to dethrone the champion. In his two previous bouts, Clay survived a razor-close decision against Doug Jones and made a trip to the canvas courtesy of a Henry Cooper left hook. Regardless of those fights, though, the 21-year-old Clay campaigned mightily for a shot against Liston.

As Clay hyped a future showdown with Liston, he wrote a poem for the occasion:

> *I predict that he will go in eight to prove that*
> *I'm great.*
> *And if he wants to go to heaven, I'll get him*
> *in seven.*
> *He'll be in a worser fix if I cut it to six.*
> *And if he keeps talking jive, I'll cut it to five.*
> *And if he makes me sore, he'll go like Archie*
> *Moore, in four.*
> *And if that don't do, I'll cut it to two.*
> *And if he run, he'll go in one.*
> *And if he don't want to fight, he should keep*
> *his ugly self home that night.*

As early as his fight against Archie Moore, Clay had been predicting he would knock Liston out in eight rounds. He and cornerman Drew "Bundini" Brown devised a camp credo—"float like a butterfly, sting like a bee"—and chanted it whenever a cameraman was nearby. Determined to spread his word, Clay bought a bus to travel cross-country and painted across the side of the vehicle: "Liston is great, but he'll fall in 8."

In July 1963, Clay gathered a small entourage, and they rode the bus to Las Vegas to witness the rematch between Liston and Patterson. Like in the first fight, Liston scored a devastating first-round knockout in the rematch. Unimpressed with Liston's power, Clay climbed into the ring afterward for an interview and exclaimed: "I want the big, ugly bear. I want the big bum as soon as I can get him. I'm tired of talking. If I can't whip that bum, I'll leave the country."

On November 5, 1963, acting against the wishes of the Louisville Sponsoring Group, who felt their fighter needed more experience, Clay signed to fight Liston in Miami Beach, Florida. His date with destiny was set: February 25, 1964.

There was good reason for the management group to be reluctant. Although Clay mocked him by calling him a "Big, Ugly Bear," Liston was considered the hardest-hitting heavyweight champ since Joe Louis. Entering the Clay fight, he had scored 13 knockouts in his 14 previous fights. He was so powerful that he could knock a man down with his left jab. But there was more to Liston than just his physical assets. He was a master at the art of intimidation. An ex-con who had served time for armed robbery and assaulting a police officer, Liston scored psychological victories by staring his opponents down before the opening bell.

Clay would not be simply challenging another man. He'd be fighting a mystique.

Liston's career began to excel when he moved to Philadelphia in the late 1950s. According to the papers filed with the Pennsylvania Athletic Commission, he was managed by Pep Barone. But Barone was merely a front man for Frank "Blinky" Palermo, a notorious mobster who, with Frankie Carbo, controlled much of

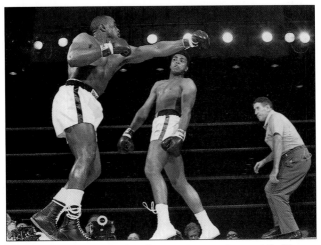

By 1964, heavyweight champ Sonny Liston (left) was past his prime and no match for the younger, quicker Clay.

boxing throughout the 1950s. Pat Duffy was a veteran manager and trainer operating in Philadelphia during Liston's prime. He promoted closed-circuit TV fights at area theaters for Liston's camp. "I was fronting for people you don't find outside of church on Sundays," said Duffy.

Duffy assisted the Liston camp in numerous ways. He chauffeured Liston to speaking engagements, and, as the manager of heavyweight Leotis Martin, he often coordinated sparring sessions between Martin and the champ. He witnessed the Liston mystique in all of its grandeur.

"Sonny Liston created a tremendous uproar after he knocked out Floyd Patterson for the second time," recalled Duffy. "At that point, I thought he was unbeat-

Ali had to be restrained by referee, and former world champion, Jersey Joe Walcott, after dropping Liston in their rematch.

able. So did almost everyone else. There weren't many heavyweights around then who were that big and that strong. Sonny's left hand was dynamite. Getting hit with it was like running into a wall. He was very difficult for another heavyweight to handle."

Liston's reputation as a brooding bully was also well earned. Despite his friendly proximity to the Liston camp, Duffy was careful not to upset the champ.

"I got along with Sonny and I liked him," said Duffy. "If he was your friend, you could have a lot of fun with the guy. But you never knew if he was gonna turn on you. He was very moody. We would be in training camp playing cards and you could have a great hand, but sometimes you'd eat it just so you wouldn't get him upset."

If fear was a major weapon in the Liston arsenal, Clay wasn't buying into it. He continued to provoke the champion. Clay was spontaneous and articulate, and his charm had become more appealing than Liston's brooding. This exchange with a TV reporter as the Liston fight drew near was a prime example that Clay's personality was contagious:

> *TV announcer: "Ladies and gentlemen, this is Cassius Marcellus Clay. He's young, he's handsome..."*
> *Clay: "They know it."*
> *The announcer grins and begins again: "He's a poet, a prophet, and many people believe he'll be the next heavyweight champion of the world. I saw Sonny Liston the other day..."*
> *Clay: "Ain't he ugly."*
> *The announcer breaks into laughter and tries to ask another question, but Clay begins talking over him.*
> *Clay: "He's too ugly to be world champion. The world champion should be pretty like me."*
> *TV announcer: "Well, he told me to bet my life that you wouldn't go three rounds."*
> *Clay: "Well, if you wanna lose your money, then bet on Sonny."*

Clay's popularity may have been rising, but few were willing to bet on him. Of the sportswriters in attendance at their fight, nearly all of them picked Liston to retain the title. In predicting Liston by knockout, Arthur Daley of *The New York Times* called Clay "a precocious master of ballyhoo" and referred to Liston as "the malefic destroyer who is champion of the world."

At the weigh-in on the morning of the fight, it appeared that the reality of meeting Liston had finally caught up with Clay. The challenger arrived wearing a jacket that had "Bear Huntin'" stenciled across the back, and he and Bundini were screaming: "Float like a butterfly, sting like a bee. Rumble, young man, rumble."

When Liston arrived, Clay went crazy. He began screaming, "I'm ready to rumble right now...I can beat you anytime, chump!" Clay was promptly fined $2,500 by the local boxing commission. When the commission doctor took Clay's blood pressure, his heart was beating at a rate of 110 beats per minute. Liston weighed in at 218 pounds, and Clay was 210 pounds. But the prevailing thought after the weigh-in was that Clay was scared.

"If you wanna lose your money, then bet on Sonny."

–Clay

Nothing was further from the truth. Just hours before he would enter the ring for the biggest fight of his life, Clay was standing in the arena cheering while his brother Rudy made his professional boxing debut. Cassius, an 8–1 underdog, seemed as confident as ever. And so did his corner.

"I knew Liston was easy to hit," recalled Angelo Dundee. "We had the right style to beat him. Liston couldn't handle all that speed."

After all the hype and histrionics, Clay was calm, composed, and confident when he arrived in the ring.

It was obvious from the outset that Liston couldn't cope with his speed. The champion was plodding after the fleet-footed Clay, attempting to club him with wide punches. Clay responded with sharp, accurate combinations.

In Round 3, Clay's combinations opened a cut on Liston's left cheekbone. But then, near the close of Round 4, Clay's eyes mysteriously began to sting. It is a common belief that liniment from Liston's shoulder or the substance used to stop his cut had somehow wound up on Clay and, mixed with Clay's sweat, trickled into his eyes. Others have floated the theory that one of Liston's cornermen purposely applied the substance to Liston's glove in an attempt to blind the challenger. Whatever the cause, Clay panicked. When he reached his corner after the round, he was blinking rapidly and screaming, "I can't see! My eyes, my eyes! Cut the gloves off. We're going home."

Dundee calmed him down, rinsed out the eyes, and, when the bell rang, ordered him to run. With his vision still obstructed, Clay endured a brutal two-fisted attack over the first half of Round 5. But, when his eyes cleared, he began to rip Sonny apart with combinations.

By Round 6, Clay assumed complete control of the fight. After that round, Liston told his corner to stop the fight. He was the first heavyweight champion since Jess Willard in 1919 to relinquish his title while sitting on his stool. The official postfight explanation was an injury to his left shoulder.

Liston's connections to organized crime led many to believe that the fight was fixed. However, there has never been any evidence to support such speculation. It went into the record books as a seventh-round TKO, and Clay would later say that Liston purposely quit at that point to ruin his prediction.

The postfight scene was bedlam, as Clay danced around the ring shouting, "I am the greatest! I shocked the world!" The new champion was consumed with euphoria, ranting incessantly about his victory and himself. As he was being interviewed on live television, with the dignified Joe Louis standing to his left, Clay ranted on: "I don't have a mark on my face," he shouted. "I must be the greatest. I upset Sonny Liston and I just turned 22 years old."

However, the world would soon say goodbye to Cassius Clay. Prior to the Liston fight, Clay started attending Nation of Islam meetings. The group was known then as Black Muslims, and their anti-white stance made them largely unpopular. When Malcolm X attended one of Clay's workouts before the Liston fight, rumors began to fester about Clay. It wasn't until after the fight that he revealed his conversion.

"I believe in the religion of Islam," *Sports Illustrated* quoted Clay after the fight. "I believe in Allah and in peace. What's wrong with that? I don't try to move into white neighborhoods. I don't want to marry a white woman. I don't want to hurt no one like the Klu Klux Klan. I was baptized when I was 12, but I didn't know what I was doing. I'm not Christian anymore."

On March 6, 1964, Nation of Islam leader Elijah Muhammad presented Clay with the name Muhammad Ali. The heavyweight champion of the world would no longer use his "slave name."

While Ali's religious conversion was the source of much controversy, that was only part of the story when he signed for a rematch against Liston in 1965. The fight was to take place in Boston, but three days before fight night, Ali underwent surgery to correct an incarcerated inguinal hernia. The rematch was postponed six months and rescheduled for May 25, 1965, in Lewiston, Maine.

Malcolm X was now distanced from the Nation of Islam, and he and Elijah Muhammad were vying for Ali's allegiance. Ali would remain loyal to the Nation. On February 21, 1965, Malcolm X was assassinated in New York. Followers of Malcolm X blamed Elijah Muhammad for the murder, and it was rumored before the Liston rematch that they would exact revenge against the Nation of Islam by assassinating Ali when he entered the ring. In the weeks leading up to the fight, Ali was under constant police protection.

Things, however, would get more bizarre on fight night. The tone was set when singer Robert Goulet forgot the words to the national anthem. When the bell rang to start the rematch, Ali began the bout dancing

Ali, flanked by brother Rudy (left) *and trainer Bundini Brown, explains the "Phantom Punch" that kayoed Liston in their rematch.*

on his toes and circling the ring. About midway through the first round, Ali landed a short, chopping right hand. Liston dropped to the canvas and chaos ensued.

Instead of going to a neutral corner, Ali stood over Liston and shouted, "Get up and fight, sucker!" Jersey Joe Walcott, the former heavyweight champ, was the referee, and he desperately tried to move Ali to a neutral corner. While that was going on, Liston had reached his knees—but then fell over again. Approximately 17 seconds after he had been knocked down, Liston rose to his feet. Walcott, who had never even issued a count, wiped Liston's gloves and allowed the fight to continue.

Somehow, Nat Fleischer, founder of *The Ring* magazine, was able to get Walcott's attention from ringside, and he informed Walcott that Liston should have been counted out. At that point, Walcott stopped the match and declared Ali the winner.

Once again, observers of the fight game cried foul. Many asserted that Liston was felled by a phantom punch. Ali has long maintained that he landed a right hand, and a video of the fight clearly supports his claim. The question, however, is whether the punch was strong enough to knock Liston out.

The only man who knows for sure was Sonny Liston. He took the truth to the grave with him when he died in 1970.

Child of the '60s

Stating that the Vietnam War conflicted with his religious beliefs, Ali refused induction into the military. His draft-evasion case dragged on in the courts from 1967 to 1971.

I f a simple word can profoundly characterize the feelings and spirit of a decade, the word for the 1960s was "fear": of subversive groups, of government, and of war. Two men helped shape the way the United States came to define fear and courage in that turbulent era: Cassius Marcellus Clay Jr., who became Muhammad Ali, the world heavyweight champion; and John Fitzgerald Kennedy, who became the 35th president of the United States but never got to go the distance.

Kennedy, a decorated hero in World War II and tragically a victim of an assassin's bullet, symbolized courage in a more traditional sense. Ali, clearly fearless in the ring, forced the country to rethink its definition of courage when he requested conscientious-objector status from the Vietnam War. At the time, that lone act was regarded by some as one of cowardice and greed. To others, though, it was a tremendous display of courage. Ali had sacrificed his title and livelihood for his principles.

In 1960, Kennedy was considered a political prodigy and Clay the prodigal son of pugilism. It was in that year that Clay, 18, returned home from the Olympics with a gold medal and Kennedy, 43, was narrowly elected over Richard Nixon to become the youngest elected president. His victory against Nixon was the closest vote ever recorded. That was a sign of the deep divisions in America and a portent of battles to come.

Clay's life was swirling. He won the Olympics, turned pro, and registered with the Selective Service System in Louisville, Kentucky. With peace at hand, Clay promptly put the registration behind him and focused on his career.

By 1962, Clay had evolved into a celebrity whose star was rising. He ran his ring record to 16–0 at the end of '62 and was becoming a force in the heavy-weight division. In contrast, the Kennedy administration was under pressure. Although Kennedy had a strong civil-rights record and had initiated the Peace Corps, the president in 1961 had weathered the Bay of Pigs invasion in Cuba and a nuclear showdown with the Russians. In 1963, the reality of war in Southeast Asia was looming.

Still, Kennedy and Clay represented that undeniable aura of youthful, we-can-make-a-difference spirit that was prevalent among young Americans in the '60s.

If the country was divided along political lines, it was also divided racially. Clay's upbringing in Louisville, where segregation was still a way of life, helped form his intense feelings on the matters of race and segregation. Those experiences likely led Clay to a religious and social connection with the Nation of Islam. Led by Elijah Muhammad and headquartered in Chicago, with branches in most of the major urban ghettos, members of the Nation of Islam were identified in the media as "Black Muslims." The teachings of Elijah Muhammad combined the traditions of orthodox Islam with black separatism. He identified whites as "blue-eyed devils," which was not taught by orthodox Muslims. Such a contradiction made it difficult for mainstream America to accept the group.

In November 1963, three months before Clay would win the title, President Kennedy was assassinated. Suddenly, a man who offered hope to so many Americans was gone. It was a pattern that would sadly repeat itself throughout the decade, with the assassi-

Although Elijah Muhammad (right) *was the Nation of Islam's leader, Ali was its most famous member.*

nations of both Robert Kennedy and Martin Luther King.

In February 1964, Clay stopped Sonny Liston to become champion of the world and announced that he would no longer be known by his "slave name," Cassius Clay. Elijah Muhammad formally gave him the name Muhammad Ali. Muhammad meant "one worthy of praise"; Ali was a general and a cousin of the Prophet Muhammad. Despite his official name change, members of the media for several years still referred to him as Cassius Clay, as did some of his opponents.

Ali was an outspoken critic of racial injustice, and his words pierced the nation's consciousness and riled his detractors in the media. However, in the African-American community, his stature was rising.

Malcolm X (left) played a major role in Ali's eventual conversion to Islam in 1964.

"Muhammad Ali offered so much hope for African-Americans," said Leon Carter, the deputy sports editor of the New York *Daily News*. "When he spoke his mind and stood up for what he believed in, I felt proud. He's one of my heroes."

As the decade began to unfold, Malcolm X, a close friend of Ali's and a charismatic speaker in the Nation of Islam, began to question its conflicts with orthodox Islam. Also gnawing at his soul were rumors of sexual liaisons and financial misconduct on the part of Elijah Muhammad. After a pilgrimage to Mecca, Malcolm X embraced orthodox Islam and changed his views of whites because he had seen "blue-eyed blonds to black-skinned Africans" worshiping and living together.

Despite the urgings of Malcolm X, Ali continued to align himself with Elijah Muhammad. Ultimately, Malcolm X's moral and ethical conflicts would cost him his life in 1965, when he was assassinated in Harlem's Audubon Ballroom.

The murder of Malcolm X—which according to supporters of Malcolm X was ordered by Elijah Muhammad—threatened Ali's safety as he prepared for the second Liston fight. It was feared that Ali might be a target of retaliation. Ali, though, won the rematch, and his career and life carried on without further threats of violence within the Black Muslim community.

Other problems would soon arise for Ali.

One month before the first Liston fight, he had been ordered to take the military written-qualifying examination. He failed, as he did the retest in March 1964. He was reclassified as not qualified under current standards. That's the way things remained until 1966.

The United States' foreign policy experts called for the military defense of South Vietnam in support of the Domino Theory, assuming that if one more country in Southeast Asia fell to communism, they all would fall. President Lyndon Johnson increased U.S. involvement in the war and reinstated the draft. At this time, the mental-aptitude requirements were lowered and, despite his attorneys' appeals, Ali was reclassified 1-A. But Ali had no intention of fighting in Vietnam.

Robert Lipsyte of *The New York Times* was in Miami with Ali when he got the news, and he was present when reporters began calling for a reaction. Lipsyte recalled that day in Thomas Hauser's biography:

"Finally, after the 10th call—'What do you think about the Vietcong?' Ali exploded. 'Man, I ain't got no quarrel with them Vietcong.' And bang. There it was. That was the headline. That was what the media wanted."

"Man, I ain't got no quarrel with them Vietcong."
—Ali

Ali was immediately criticized in the media. Sports columnist Jimmy Cannon wrote: "Clay is part of the Beatle movement. He fits in with the famous singers no one can hear and the punks riding motorcycles with iron crosses pinned to their leather jackets and Batman and the boys with their long dirty hair and the girls with the unwashed look and the college kids dancing naked at secret proms held in apartments and the revolt of the students who get a check from Dad every first of the month and the painters who copy the labels off soup cans and the surf bums who refuse to

Martin Luther King (right) supported Ali's stance on refusing to serve in the Army.

work and the whole pampered style-making cult of the bored young."

Cannon's assessment of Ali and his era was harsh. But rarely had an athlete been so outspoken, so aware of social issues. Cannon and his brethren in the sporting press were accustomed to athletes who restricted their comments to what transpired during athletic contests. They were also accustomed to athletes who were patriotic. Even beloved heavyweight champion Jack Dempsey, one of the most popular athletes of this century, was labeled a "slacker" after he was given a draft deferment from World War I. Dempsey later made amends when, in his 40s, he served in the Coast Guard during World War II.

But not since the Civil War had the United States fought a war that an increasing number of its citizens did not support.

In the wake of the Ali controversy, comparisons were immediately drawn between him and former heavyweight champion Joe Louis, of whom Cannon once wrote: "Joe Louis is a credit to his race, the human race." Louis volunteered for the United States Army during World War II, as did most boxing champions—and most American men for that matter. Louis fought numerous exhibitions to entertain troops, and he donated some of his championship purses to the United States Army Relief Fund. Like Louis, it's doubtful that Ali would have seen any combat.

"A lot of the criticism leveled at Ali had to do with his race," said Carter. "This was an era of racial unrest. At that time, the only areas that blacks were successful in were athletics and entertainment. People would

By 1966, Ali's religious beliefs and his stance on the draft had made him the most controversial athlete in America.

cheer you on the field, but for the most part the white media wasn't interested in what a black man believed."

In August 1966, Ali's appeal for reclassification was upheld by a retired Kentucky State Circuit Court judge, who ruled that Ali was sincere in his objection on religious grounds. However, the Department of Justice wrote a report to the Appeals Board opposing the decision, arguing that his opposition was political and racial and that his beliefs were a matter of convenience and opportunity.

In the midst of the controversy, Ali complicated matters further when he fought Ernie Terrell on February 6, 1967. Terrell refused to call the champion Muhammad Ali and referred to him as Cassius Clay. For that transgression, Ali humiliated Terrell. Throughout the course of the bout, Ali repeatedly asked his opponent "what's my name?" as he peppered him with punches. Ali punished Terrell for 15 brutal rounds. When it was over, and Terrell was left bloodied and battered, the media was left wondering what kind of minister was capable of such a nasty, premeditated beating.

Then, one month later, the National Selective Service Presidential Appeal Board voted unanimously to maintain Ali's 1-A classification. He received his order to report for induction in Houston on April 28. Though he had returned to boxing business as usual, defeating Zora Folley at Madison Square Garden, Ali was no less resolute in his position outside the ring.

Ali joined 26 other young men reporting for induction that day. After filling out forms and taking physicals, it was time to step forward and be sworn into the military. Ali refused and, when asked to write down his refusal, did so, stating, "I refuse to be inducted into the armed forces of the United States because I claim to be exempt as a minister of religion for Islam."

The response was immediate and severe. The New York State Athletic Commission stripped Ali of his title and refused to license him to fight further in New York. As New York went, so did the rest of the country's state boxing authorities. Ten days after refusing induction, Ali was indicted by a Federal Grand Jury in Houston, arrested, photographed, fingerprinted, and released on $5,000 bail.

Ali's trial began on June 19, 1967. Jury selection took one day. Witnesses were heard and evidence was submitted on the second day, and by 5:50 P.M. the case went to an all-white jury. Twenty minutes later, they came back with a guilty verdict. Ali asked the judge to pronounce his sentence immediately. The U.S. attorney was heard from and recommended less than the maximum. Nevertheless, the judge imposed the maximum allowed: five years and a fine of $10,000.

The judge confiscated Ali's passport. Since he couldn't get licensed in America, his career in the prize ring was terminated. Life, however, continued. Ali appealed the ruling, and in the meantime he became a rousing speaker on college campuses.

Then, on June 28, 1971, 50 months to the day after Ali had refused induction, the U.S. Supreme Court unanimously reversed his conviction. All pending criminal charges were dismissed. Now it was time to reclaim the heavyweight title.

CHAPTER 6

Exile

*In 1967, Ali was on top of the world—29–0
with nine consecutive title defenses. That spring,
however, he was banished from the ring for his
antiwar stance, robbing 3½ years from his prime.*

T he best Muhammad Ali is the one we never
saw." Those are the words of Angelo Dundee,
who served as Ali's trainer for over 20 years.
Having been so close to Ali for so long, he possesses
the most intimate knowledge of Ali's vast talent. He
witnessed Ali's progression from preliminary fighter to
world champion.

The time period Dundee speaks of ranges from
March 23, 1967, to October 25, 1970. Over that course
of time, Ali did not engage in a real fight. As a result
of his refusal to serve in the United States Army, Ali
was absent from the ring at the precise moment he
had reached his physical peak. Ironically, Ali's exile is
similar in timing to Ted Williams's active military service during World War II. In 1941, the 23-year-old

Ali received heavy criticism for his perceived "torture" of former champ Floyd Patterson, who he easily outclassed in their November 1966 grudge match.

Williams batted .406 for the Boston Red Sox. In 1943, he was in the Air Force and didn't return to baseball until 1946.

How many home runs might Williams have hit had he not twice interrupted his career for military service? How many great fights would Ali have had if he had not been banned from boxing for his antiwar stance? Such questions will forever haunt sports fans.

To fully understand what the boxing world missed out on, first consider Ali's rapid ascension after knocking out Sonny Liston in their May 1965 rematch. Ali's next title defense came against former champion Floyd Patterson on November 22, 1965. Immediately, Ali dubbed Patterson "The Rabbit" because he claimed the veteran was scared to fight. The prefight hype seemed innocent enough until Patterson took a jab at the Nation of Islam and made the claim that he was going to win the heavyweight title back for America. The counter was Ali at his worst, or—depending upon one's views—his best. He recited a poem that read:

> I'm gonna put him flat on his back,
> So that he will start acting black.
> Because when he was champ he didn't do as
> he should.
> He tried to force himself into an all-white
> neighborhood.

The fight was never competitive. Ali dropped Patterson with a jab and dominated the action. It seemed Ali could have won at any moment, but he allowed the fight to go into the 12th round before it was stopped. When it was over, Ali was harshly criticized for prolonging the fight just so he could punish Patterson.

Shortly after the Patterson fight, Ali's draft status was reclassified. Suddenly, he was faced with the possibility of going to Vietnam. He made it clear, though, that war was not part of his future when he said, "I ain't got no quarrel with them Vietcong."

With the draft controversy already swirling, Ali's fight against WBA heavyweight champion Ernie Terrell was in jeopardy. The bout was scheduled for Chicago but, bowing to pressure from newspapers and local politicians, the Illinois Athletic Commission canceled the contest. Terrell then pulled out when the fight was moved from Chicago, his hometown, to Toronto, Canada. The replacement opponent was tough Canadian heavyweight George Chuvalo, who accepted the fight on 17 days' notice.

The fight took place in Toronto's Maple Leaf Gardens on March 29, 1966. Ali predicted that he would be the first man to send Chuvalo to the canvas. He was wrong. The granite-chinned Chuvalo remained standing for the entire 15 rounds as Ali won a unanimous decision. Afterwards, Ali told reporters, "Chuvalo's head is the hardest thing I ever punched."

"Chuvalo's head is the hardest thing I ever punched."
—Ali

Ali then took his title to Europe. The first stop was London, where he would engage in a May 21 rematch with Henry Cooper. It was the first time England had hosted a heavyweight title fight since 1908. The fact that Cooper floored the champion in their first fight provided British boxing fans a glimmer of hope for the return encounter. A crowd of 46,000 fans attended the contest at Arsenal Stadium. All hope was dashed in Round 6 when an Ali cross opened a terrible cut above Cooper's left eye. The contest was stopped at 1:38 of the round. Ten weeks later, Ali defended his title against another Englishman. This time, he knocked out Brian London in the third round.

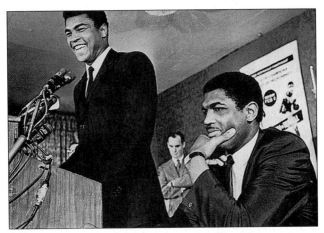

Although Ali joked with Ernie Terrell at this press conference, he issued a terrible beating to the challenger, who insisted on calling him Clay.

Ali concluded his European tour with a defense against German Karl Mildenberger before 45,000 fans in Frankfurt, Germany, on September 10. The fight is historic only because Mildenberger became the first southpaw to challenge for the heavyweight title in the 20th century. While Mildenberger proved to be a worthy adversary over the first four rounds, Ali took control of the fight by dropping him with a right hand in Round 5. He scored two more knockdowns before the bout was halted in the 11th round.

It has been suggested by numerous boxing experts that Ali was at his absolute peak during the Cleveland Williams fight. In fact, Howard Cosell told author Thomas Hauser that, on that night, Ali was "the most devastating fighter who ever lived." The bout took place on November 14, 1966, in the Houston Astrodome before 35,460 fans. It was also during this match that the Ali shuffle was born.

At one time, Williams was considered the hardest puncher in the heavyweight division. However, at age 33 and having recovered from a gunshot wound, Williams was no longer the feared contender who had wreaked havoc on the division.

From the opening bell, Ali glided across the ring with the grace and fluidity of a gold-medal figure skater. While Williams struggled to reach his elusive opponent, Ali's blinding left jab was scoring with alarming frequency. In the second round, Ali unleashed a flurry of power punches. He dropped Williams three times in that round and scored another knockdown in the third. At the 1:08 mark of Round 3, referee Harry Kessler stopped the fight.

Zora Folley, Ali's last opponent before his three-year banishment, is kayoed in Round 4, March 1967.

Twelve weeks later, Ali returned to the Astrodome to finally meet Terrell. Ali again revealed a nastiness that disturbed even the hardest of ringside observers. While Ali routinely made up names for his opponents, Terrell decided to play the name game himself and refused to call him Ali. Terrell referred to him as Cassius Clay. That incited Ali, who told the press Cassius Clay was his slave name.

At the time, Terrell was considered Ali's toughest opponent since Liston. Standing 6'6", he possessed an 82-inch reach and an excellent left jab. He was unbeaten over the previous five years and had scored victories over Doug Jones, Chuvalo, and Williams.

Ali promised to punish his opponent, and that's exactly what he did. Ali controlled the action over 15 one-sided rounds, shouting "What's my name?" at Terrell while distributing a lopsided beating. Terrell's face was swollen, and he suffered a fracture of the cheekbone beneath his left eye.

Then on March 22, 1967, Ali was back in the ring against 34-year-old contender Zora Folley. Once again, Ali was dominant, scoring a seventh-round knockout at Madison Square Garden. It was Ali's ninth successful title defense. He had cleaned out the heavyweight division, and it could be argued that he didn't lose a round in the process.

Few realized at the time that it could have been Ali's last fight.

Ali was 25 years old and had a record of 29–0 with 23 knockouts. He was on top of the world. But it was a world that would come crashing down on April 28, 1967, when he refused induction into the United States Army. Muhammad was stripped of his boxing license and his heavyweight title.

Ali did not return to the ring until the fall of 1970. While most believe Ali was at his best just before he was exiled, the opinions do vary among boxing experts. Chuvalo is one of two men to fight Ali before and after the exile (Patterson was the other). Chuvalo offers this assessment:

> **"The first time we fought, he thought he was God in the ring. Everything was working for him. Everything he did was right. He felt he could knock anyone out.**
>
> **—George Chuvalo**

"The first Ali was better, period," said the Canadian. "He was younger and quicker. When I fought him in 1972, he realized his limitations to some degree. I don't think he did in 1966. He was still riding that wave of youthful exuberance.

"The first time we fought, he thought he was God in the ring. Everything was working for him. Everything he did was right. He felt he could knock anyone out. He wasn't forever young when he came back. Things had chipped away at him a little bit. He had lost to Frazier and he went through everything with the draft. When I fought him the second time, he was smarter. But I was smarter, too. I was stronger the first time, but smarter the second. I did things differently in the fight.

"I saw Ali at his best. I fought him in '66. I was in Houston when he fought Cleveland Williams. I saw him fight Zora Folley. Ali was at his absolute best right before the exile."

Dave Anderson is one of only three sportswriters in history to win a Pulitzer Prize. He writes a sports column for *The New York Times* and covered Ali's boxing career from start to finish.

"Ali was faster before the exile," said Anderson. "To me, one was Cassius Clay, so to speak, and later Muhammad Ali. Even though he changed his name earlier, that's the way I think of him. Almost like he had two careers. So the question is, could Cassius Clay beat Muhammad Ali? I would say that Ali would win because he was bigger, stronger, and had more experience."

Al Gavin is one of the foremost cutmen in boxing. Throughout his career, he has worked with three heavyweight champions and one-time Ali opponent Chuck Wepner.

"He was better before the exile," said Gavin. "He was younger and he was faster. Later he put on weight, and that affected his speed. He was also a little more subdued after he came back.

"Before he won the title, he fought Billy Daniels, Sonny Banks, and Doug Jones. Those were great fights because Ali had to use all his skills to win them. And he had plenty of skills. Then he became champion and it seemed he just kept getting better. To me, he was at his peak when they took the title away from him."

Hall of Fame referee Arthur Mercante was a fixture on the big-fight scene for over a decade. Based in New York, Mercante refereed numerous heavyweight title fights, including three of Ali's post-exile contests.

"He was just as good or better after the layoff," said Mercante. "Before the layoff, you had a great fighter in there with guys he was superior to. After the comeback, he fought much better competition. I'm convinced he was a better fighter after the layoff."

Tom Kenville was a publicist for Madison Square Garden during Ali's prime. He worked Ali's fight against Folley and many of his fights after the exile, including the first Ali-Frazier fight and the third Ali-Norton bout.

"Muhammad was gone for 42 months," said Kenville. "There is no telling what would have happened. Muhammad lost all that time in his prime. You just don't know what might have been. He was so fast, the fastest heavyweight I had seen. He might have lost some Muhammad Ali speed when he came back, but he was still faster than any other heavyweight around.

"The one thing that stands out in my mind after he came back is his size. He was so much bigger when he came back. He was a fully developed man. You noticed how broad and imposing he was. Still...there was just no way he could be as good as he was before he left."

The Fight of the Century

For the first time in history, an undefeated heavyweight champion, Joe Frazier, met an undefeated former champ, Ali. It was the most anticipated boxing match in 33 years.

I t was called "The Fight of the Century," and it was not an exaggeration. Over-hyped fights often do not live up to their billing. But when Muhammad Ali met "Smokin' Joe" Frazier at Madison Square Garden on March 8, 1971, it was so much more than a heavyweight championship fight. To this day, its title remains appropriate.

The first Ali-Frazier fight transcended the sport of boxing. Its significance crossed social, political, and racial lines. It pitted Ali, the defiant child of the 1960s, against Frazier, the humble, hard-working champion. At the time, a large portion of mainstream America still viewed Ali as a draft-dodging Muslim. He was not considered a hero but a coward who was to be held in contempt. Ali, though, did have his loyal fans. He developed a cultlike following among the younger people of that generation and rode a wave of antiwar sentiment into the bout. Still unbeaten inside a ring, Ali proclaimed himself "the people's champion."

Frazier was much more subdued, and because he was not outspoken about politics or religion, the media—with some prodding by Ali—painted him as "the establishment's champion." It was not a title he gravitated to, but it seemed fitting nonetheless. Frazier was a Bible-reading, blue-collar fighter whose low-key approach to his craft was admired by numerous fans worldwide.

This fight was absolutely the most anticipated heavyweight title fight since Joe Louis knocked out Max Schmeling in the first round of their 1938 rematch at Yankee Stadium. The outcome of Ali-Frazier would be debated in corporate boardrooms, factories, suburban country clubs, and ghetto street corners. In the war of words that preceded the fight, Ali's verbal jabs landed early and often. "It will be no contest," he promised. "There's no way I can lose."

On paper, Ali and Frazier seemed an even match. They were both former Olympic champions. Ali won the light-heavyweight gold medal in 1960, and Frazier captured the heavyweight gold in 1964. As professionals, they both entered the ring with undefeated records. Ali was 31–0 with 25 knockouts, while Frazier was 26–0 with 23 KOs. This fight marked the first time in history that an unbeaten former champion would face an unbeaten champion for the heavyweight title. Frazier had assumed the throne as heavyweight king, and Ali was eager to take back his title. At the time, Floyd Patterson was the only man ever to win the heavyweight title twice.

In Ali's mind, there was one clear favorite—him.

"Joe Frazier is too ugly to be champ," he told reporters. "Joe Frazier is too dumb to be champ. The heavyweight champion should be smart and pretty like me."

Ali even constructed a poem about the fight:

> *Joe's gonna come out Smokin',*
> *But I ain't gonna be jokin'.*
> *I'll be peckin' and pokin',*
> *Pouring water in his smokin'.*
> *This may shock and amaze ya,*
> *But I'm gonna destroy Joe Frazier.*

Frazier was 27 years old and in the midst of his prime. He had made six successful title defenses, five coming by knockout. Ali was 29 years old and had just two tuneup fights after three years of inactivity. He returned to the ring with a third-round TKO of Jerry Quarry on October 26, 1970. Then he stopped Oscar Bonavena in the 15th round of a grueling fight on December 7, 1970. Immediately following that fight, he agreed to fight Frazier three months later. Was there enough time to recover from Bonavena and prepare for Frazier?

"I thought Muhammad took the fight too soon," said Dr. Ferdie Pacheco, Ali's personal physician and cornerman. "I would have liked to wait four or five months. He needed a solid rest. The Bonavena fight was a very tough fight; Muhammad took tremendous punishment to the body. There was no hurry to make the Frazier fight. It was the only fight out there. There was time; they could have let the gate and the anticipation build."

Joe Frazier (right) *doesn't appear to be amused by Ali's antics.*

It was indeed the only fight out there, and perhaps that was the reason it was made in such a hurry. The bout was promoted by boxing neophytes Jerry Perenchio and Jack Kent Cooke. Madison Square Garden bid a $1.25 million guarantee or 35 percent of the fight's gross, whichever figure was greater. But the Garden was outbid by Perenchio, head of a Hollywood management firm that handled Marlin Brando and Elizabeth Taylor, and Cooke, who owned the Los Angeles Lakers and Kings. They guaranteed each fighter $2.5 million, a record for purses at the time.

Cooke wanted the fight to take place at L.A.'s Great Western Forum. But Frazier, who made four title defenses at the Garden, demanded it take place in New York. The Garden was sold out a full month before the fight, and ringside tickets were going for a record $150. At the time, scalpers were getting as much as $700 per ticket.

Ali's incessant bombast turned the fight into a happening. The hype turned ugly, though, when Ali branded Frazier an Uncle Tom and predicted that most of white America would root for Frazier. He went a step further when he was quoted as saying, "Any black person who is for Joe Frazier is a traitor." While Ali would later claim he was just trying to build up the fight, someone took his taunts very seriously: Frazier received death threats before the fight and was under constant guard by New York City detectives.

"Neither fighter trained in New York for the fight, so we would give the New York writers daily updates from Frazier's camp in Philadelphia and Ali's camp in Miami," said Tom Kenville, the Garden's longtime boxing publicist. "But we didn't have to build up this fight. The Garden was already sold-out. No one had to sell the public on a fight between Ali and Frazier."

Finally, the time for fighting arrived.

"I've never seen anything like it before or since," said Frazier's cornerman, Eddie Futch, whose career in boxing spanned seven decades. "I'm glad I had the opportunity to be close to it."

Ringside at the Garden throbbed with celebrities. Actor Burt Lancaster was part of a broadcast team that included Hall of Famer Don Dunphy and former light-heavyweight champion Archie Moore. Barbra Streisand, Bill Cosby, Sammy Davis Jr., and Hugh Hefner, with a Playboy bunny at his side, were just a few of the celebrities who were in attendance. John

Condon, the late head of public relations for the Garden, even had to chase Dustin Hoffman and Diana Ross out of the working press section. There were 760 press credentials issued for the fight, and another 500 requests were denied.

"After I was asked to enter the ring, it took about 12 or 15 minutes before the atmosphere sunk in," said Arthur Mercante, who refereed the fight. "I looked out into the crowd, and as far as you could see there were Hollywood personalities, local politicians, national politicians. Toots Shor came with two busloads of his customers, and they were all dressed in formal attire. Gene Tunney and Jack Dempsey were there. It was an electric evening."

There would still be one more celebrity surprise that would forever add to the mystique of this fight.

"The working press section was huge, and it was already filled when they turned the lights down for the national anthem," recalled Kenville. "All of a sudden, when the lights went on, there was Frank Sinatra. He was in a neutral corner in seat number 43. I couldn't believe it, but it was him, 'Ol' Blue Eyes.' He was taking pictures for *Life* magazine. John Condon had to walk him in while the lights were out so it didn't cause a big commotion."

They say that styles make fights, and there were never two styles—two fighters—more perfect for each other. Ali was the boxer, Frazier the puncher. It is a formula that has served matchmakers well for decades. Boxers will always be paired with punchers, but few will ever go toe-to-toe the way Ali and Frazier did. Ali was fast, fluid, and flamboyant. Frazier was a warrior with a wrecking ball for a left hook. Simply put, Ali and Frazier brought the best out of each other.

"Muhammad Ali was a great performer and a great fighter," said Futch, the architect of Frazier's winning fight plan. "But like most great fighters, he had a flaw. They do things a certain way for so long that when you start to take advantage of that flaw, they can't drop the habit. I knew this about Ali. I watched him in many fights. I knew you could take advantage of his weakness and he'd never correct it because it was part of him. He wasn't going to stop what he was doing for just one fight. It had been successful his whole career, so why stop?

"I knew that Ali pulled straight back from punches. And I knew he didn't like to throw uppercuts. When he threw one, he had no way to escape the counter-punch. Now, he was so quick that most fighters couldn't take advantage of that. Ali didn't throw the uppercut often, but when he did he threw it standing straight up. That left him defenseless. To entice Ali, I made Joe get lower, to get into a deeper crouch. That forced him to throw the uppercut. Then I told Joe to go over the top of the uppercut with a left hook."

The first punches thrown—almost simultaneously—were a left hook by Frazier and a jab by Ali. That pattern held true for nearly the entire 15 rounds. Ali jabbing and throwing one-twos, and Frazier sweeping that devastating hook toward Ali's head or ribs.

Ali weighed in at 215 pounds while Frazier scaled 205½. It seemed from the outset that Ali's hand and foot speed had diminished slightly from his prime. Perhaps that is why Ali chose to fight flatfooted. He no longer floated like a butterfly, but he was content to simply confront Frazier.

"That was the only way Muhammad could have fought him," said Pacheco. "If Muhammad got up on his toes and danced, he would have been exhausted after five or six rounds. Frazier would have been all over him. Muhammad was a master at knowing how to use his body. He knew he couldn't dance all night. People think he could do that and not get tired. But it is tiring."

Ali edged backward for much of the fight, snapping left-right combinations, while Frazier burrowed forward, ripping hooks to the head and body. The champion seemed to counter every Ali punch with a potent hook. Ali was able to pull back from some, but not all. And when Frazier was not head-hunting, he was driving hard lefts and rights into Ali's midsection.

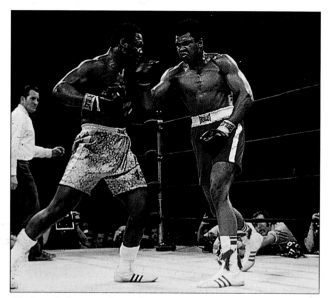

Ali landed countless clean punches, but they could not stop the ever-charging champion.

The pace was so fierce that Dunphy, the legendary voice of boxing who called numerous heavyweight title fights, said, "This is the most torrid heavyweight championship fight of all time."

Ali talked to Frazier through much of the bout, and Mercante warned him several times to stop chattering. One exchange went like this:

Ali: "Don't you know I'm God?"

Frazier: "God, you are in the wrong place tonight."

Still, Ali talked and talked and mugged to the crowd. Each time Frazier landed a hard punch, Ali looked out into the audience and shook his head, as if to say, "That didn't hurt."

Ali predicted a sixth-round knockout, but when that round arrived it was Frazier who came out smokin'. He battered Ali to the ropes, and the former champ seemed content to stay there. Once Ali would have danced away, but on this night he absorbed Frazier's bombs while resting on the ropes. Ali offered only token resistance, as Frazier pounded away. It was almost surreal as Ali tapped Frazier with light blows to the forehead, almost as if he were knocking on a door. The fight was beginning to slip away from Ali.

"Muhammad permitted himself to be hit needlessly," remembered Mercante. "And he threw those pitter-patter punches. He just gave away rounds."

Ali again retreated to the ropes in Round 8 and offered more "pitter-patter" punches. Mercante implored him to fight as the crowd began to boo. Suddenly, Frazier grabbed Ali by the arms and pulled him toward the center of the ring so the fighting could resume. That prompted Dunphy to comment, "I don't know anyone who gets the sheer joy of combat that Joe Frazier does."

Just when it seemed Ali would concede victory, he emerged in the ninth round ready to take back his title. He fired piercing left-right combinations, and for the first time in the fight Frazier took a backward step. They continued that way until it ended, each one possessing a fierce determination to win. This was no longer a sporting event; it was personal. And among the great champions of this sport, pride always counts more than money or title belts.

The fight turned again in what the Ali camp forever refers to as the "terrible 11th." With 49 seconds left in that round, Ali was stunned by a Smokin' Joe hook. A second hook buckled Ali's knees, and he collapsed into the ropes. With 30 seconds remaining, Ali slid out of the corner and began taunting Frazier, concealing the fact that he was truly hurt. With 18 seconds left in the round, Ali stumbled backward across the ring into the ropes. Frazier hesitated briefly before walking after him. When he arrived, he fired yet another hook. The bell, however, rescued Ali.

> ## "No one had ever hurt Muhammad before. Not Liston, no one. After that round, after this fight, we knew we had a guy with guts."
> ### –Dr. Ferdie Pacheco

"I was thinking that it was a miracle he survived that round," recalled Pacheco. "No one had ever hurt Muhammad before. Not Liston, no one. After that round, after this fight, we knew we had a guy with guts."

Frazier's trademark left hook sent Ali crashing to the canvas for a four-count in the 15th round.

Futch offered this view from the Frazier corner: "Joe hurt Ali badly in the 11th round with a left hook. But he conned Joe into thinking he wasn't hurt. We still tease Joe about that. We call it the long march, because Joe walked across the ring after Ali .... He was able to fight Joe off until the fight ended."

Ali recovered from the beating in the 11th round and came out a determined warrior for the 15th and final round. The effects of battle were written on Frazier's swollen face. But pain was not a deterrent in this fight. At the 2:34 mark, Ali began to throw a right uppercut. Just as Futch predicted, Ali's head was unguarded. Frazier responded with a left hook and—boom!—Ali crashed onto the seat of his red-velvet trunks. The red-and-white tassels that adorned Ali's boxing shoes fluttered in the air as his legs lifted off the ground.

But Ali rose almost as quickly as he went down.

"I was sitting about two feet from where Ali landed," recalled Dave Anderson, *The New York Times'* Pulitzer Prize-winning sports columnist. "When he hit the canvas, it sounded like a clap of thunder. Frazier hit him with a tremendous left hook. But the thing that impressed me most was how quickly Ali got up. He got up as quickly as you can get up from a knockdown."

Amazingly, Ali had survived the round, though the fight was already lost. The decision was unanimous. Mercante's scorecard was the closest. He had it eight rounds for Frazier, six for Ali, and one even. Judge Artie Aidala had it nine rounds to six, and judge Bill Recht scored it 11 to four, both in favor of Frazier.

"John Condon asked me to bring Ali to the postfight press conference," said Kenville. "The Garden was still emptying, and I fought my way to his dressing room. It was like a morgue in there. Ali had already gone to the hospital to have his jaw X-rayed. I needed someone to come to the press conference, so Bundini Brown agreed to go. I'll never forget his opening line when he reached the podium. 'Well, I guess you all got what you were looking for,' he said. Bundini was referring to that fact that Ali was still the villain and Frazier was the good guy."

The fight was witnessed by 20,455 spectators at the Garden, and an estimated 300 million more worldwide watched it on closed-circuit television. The live gate generated $1.3 million, and the closed-circuit sales generated another $25 million. At that time, the biggest closed-circuit bout had been the first match between Sonny Liston and Floyd Patterson, which generated $3.2 million.

"Joe was at his best that night," said Kenville. "It would have been hard for anyone to have beaten him. Maybe Rocky Marciano could have matched him in strength for 15 rounds. And maybe Joe Louis would have been able to hold him off. But Joe was on a mission. He took some terrific punches by Ali, but he was indestructible that night."

There are several factors that set this fight apart from all other heavyweight championships. The first was the political climate of the era, which offered Ali a platform to express his views. The second was that both men entered the ring undefeated and equally matched. Ultimately, though, what made the first Ali-Frazier fight distinctive was the way they fought each other. Not their styles, but their desire. Frazier was fueled by pride and, perhaps, a genuine hatred for Ali. Ali was motivated to prove he was indeed "The Greatest."

It was a supreme effort by both men, and they left nothing behind after 15 rounds. They gave it all to the fans and to the sport of boxing. All heavyweight championship fights will be judged against the standard that Ali and Frazier set at Madison Square Garden on March 8, 1971.

Boxing may never see another night like it.

The Road Back

After he lost the 1971 title fight to Joe Frazier, Ali still took on the best the world had to offer. Over the next three years, he fought four one-time heavyweight champions.

Oftentimes, when a fighter of this era loses his first fight, the immediate strategy is to line him up a series of confidence-building fights. Today's managers and promoters often force-feed their fighters a steady diet of tomato cans—opponents who have virtually no chance at winning—until they return to their lofty stature in the ratings. It is a trend that is damaging the sport of boxing and an indication from the promoters and managers that may suggest they have lost confidence in their fighters.

Even in defeat, Muhammad Ali never lost his confidence. He had no use for tomato cans. After Joe Frazier handed Ali his first professional loss in March 1971, Ali was back in the ring a little more than four months later. The opponent was his longtime friend and former World Boxing Association (WBA) heavy-weight champion Jimmy Ellis. While Ali still figured to beat most heavyweights in the division's Top 10, he clearly wasn't taking the easy road back to the top.

From the time he lost to Frazier until the time he regained the heavyweight title three years later, Ali fought 14 times. Of those opponents, eight were ranked in the heavyweight division's Top 10. Of those eight, three had been heavyweight champion and one would go on to win the heavyweight title. Yet another, Bob Foster, was the reigning light-heavyweight champion and a future Hall of Famer.

The Ellis fight took place on July 26, 1971, in the Houston Astrodome. At stake was the North American Boxing Federation (NABF) heavyweight title. Ellis was raised in Louisville, and he and Ali started boxing at the same gym under the tutelage of Joe Martin. The pair remained friends and Ellis eventually began training in Miami with Angelo Dundee, often serving as Ali's sparring partner. At first, Ellis turned pro as a middleweight and enjoyed moderate success. By 1966, he had grown into a full-fledged heavyweight, and two years later, with Ali in exile, he captured the WBA heavyweight crown with a decision over Jerry Quarry.

Friendships have long prevented some of boxing's best matchups from occurring. Rocky Graziano and Jake LaMotta never fought because of their relationship outside the ring. The same could be said for Joe Frazier and Ken Norton, a matchup that is conspicuously absent from the great heavyweight showdowns from the 1970s.

The promoters hyped the Ali-Ellis match as "The Inevitable Meeting." Yet the fight posed difficult problems for all parties, including Dundee. With Ali's permission, Dundee worked Ellis's corner in the Astrodome, marking the first time in 10 years that Ali fought without Angelo.

With countless rounds of sparring experience to draw on, Ellis entered the ring confident of victory. There was nothing Ali could do that would surprise him. As a former middleweight, Ellis still possessed enough speed to keep pace with Ali. But sparring and actually fighting were as different as facing a batting-practice pitcher and Sandy Koufax. Ali controlled the fight with his jab and rattled Ellis occasionally with right hands. Several reporters criticized Ali's performance, arguing that he let up on Ellis when he clearly could have knocked him out. Finally, one of Ali's right hands wobbled Ellis in the 12th round, and a follow-up barrage forced referee Jay Edson to stop the fight.

Ali closed out the 1971 campaign with a November 17 decision over Buster Mathis in the Astrodome and a seventh-round knockout of Jurgen Blin in Zurich, Switzerland, on the day after Christmas. Mathis, once a formidable contender who had fought Joe Frazier for the vacant title in 1968, was far past his prime. Ali's slogan for the bout was "I'm gonna do to Buster what the Indians did to Custer." He scored two knockdowns in the 12th round and won a lopsided decision. Six weeks later, in what was his first fight in Europe since 1966, Ali knocked out the overmatched Blin.

Ali's road show continued through 1972. He met the hard-hitting Mac Foster on April 1 in Tokyo, Japan. Foster had scored 28 knockouts in compiling a 28–1 record, but he was no match for Ali, who won a unanimous 15-round decision. Ali then notched a

In their September 1973 rematch, Ali again beat Floyd Patterson, via seventh-round knockout. Patterson retired after the bout.

12-round win over George Chuvalo in Vancouver, British Columbia, before returning home to stop Quarry in seven rounds in Las Vegas.

Just one month after the Quarry fight, Ali fought again. He knocked out Al "Blue" Lewis in the 11th round of a fight held in Dublin, Ireland. Ali won over local boxing fans when he informed them that his maternal great grandfather was a man named Abe Grady, who emigrated to the United States from County Clare, Ireland.

Ali ended the year with knockout wins over former heavyweight king Floyd Patterson (KO 7) and reigning light-heavyweight champ Bob Foster (KO 8). Still, he showed no signs of slowing down. On Valentine's Day 1973, Muhammad scored a 12-round decision over formidable contender Joe Bugner in Las Vegas for his 10th consecutive victory. Ali entered the ring that night with a jewel-studded robe that had "People's Champion" stenciled across the back. The robe was a gift from Elvis Presley.

Ali was cruising along the comeback trail when he signed to fight Ken Norton, a relatively unknown heavyweight from San Diego.

Then the unthinkable happened. Ali, a 5–1 favorite, lost.

Most people knew very little about Norton. A former U.S. Marine and college football player, Norton built a 29-1 record against second-tier opposition. Ali trained just three weeks for the fight, and those training sessions were hampered after he sprained an ankle while playing golf.

Once again, the architect behind Ali's defeat was trainer Eddie Futch. Futch, who helped plan Frazier's strategy, had come up with a brilliant fight plan for Norton. Futch had tremendous respect for Ali's left jab.

Ali fought on valiantly against Ken Norton, despite suffering a broken jaw in Round 2 of their March 1973 fight.

He knew it was fast, he knew it was stiff, and he knew it was the key to Ali's entire offensive arsenal. But Norton himself possessed a good left jab, so Futch decided to match jabs with the master.

"I told Kenny to go after Ali with his jab," said Futch. "When Ali jabs, you jab. That will offset Ali's balance and rhythm."

There was one other wrinkle to Futch's strategy. The trainer noticed that Ali fell into a habit of sitting on the ropes. He advised Norton that whenever Ali retreated to the ropes, "don't go for the hook to the head. When you get to the ropes, go to the body immediately and make him bring his elbows down to block those punches." Once Ali did that, his head would be wide open for a right hand.

"I wasn't an underdog. I was lower than that before the first fight," said Norton. "But at the time, with Eddie Futch in my corner, and the shape I was in, I didn't think anyone would beat me that night. It would have been totally impossible."

The course of the fight was decided in the second round when a Norton right hand broke Ali's jaw. Ali showed tremendous courage by fighting the remaining 10 rounds at a fast pace. But Norton, 29 years old, never wavered from Futch's plan. He matched Ali jab for jab and pummeled the former champ's body whenever he retreated to the ropes.

The fight was close entering the last round, and Norton outhustled Ali over the final three minutes to earn a split decision and the biggest win of his career. Norton had become the NABF champion.

Ali underwent a 90-minute operation to repair his jaw and was idle for six months—until he met Norton again on September 10, 1973.

The rematch took place at the Great Western Forum in Inglewood, California. Once again, the fight would take place on the West Coast, where Norton's following was at its strongest. But that seemed like little consolation to Norton.

"Ali is at home wherever he fights," he said. "You could fight him in your own backyard and the crowd would be on Ali's side."

> "Ali is at home wherever he fights. You could fight him in your own backyard and the crowd would be on Ali's side."
> –Ken Norton

Ali controlled the first half of the fight by jabbing and moving. But as he started to tire in the middle and late rounds, Norton increased his body attack and began to find a home for his own left jab.

"In the second fight, Norton made a dumb mistake," recalled Futch. "He decided that he could fight like Joe Frazier. I jumped all over him and got him to fight like Ken Norton should fight by the fifth round. Ali still got the decision, but it was close."

Once again, the fight was decided in the 12th and final round. This time, it was Ali who controlled the final three minutes of the fight and was awarded a close unanimous decision.

Six weeks later, Ali was back in the ring. He decisioned the unheralded Rudi Lubbers over 12 rounds in Jakarta, Indonesia. It was his 13th bout since losing "The Fight of the Century." Finally, it was time to settle a score with Joe Frazier.

The Ali-Frazier rematch lacked some of the appeal of their first match. Ali had been beaten by Norton, and Frazier had suffered a devastating second-round knockout at the hands of the new champion, George Foreman. The bout was held on January 28, 1974, before a sellout crowd at Madison Square Garden, which at the time was still the mecca of boxing. Although he was a slight underdog in their first fight, Ali was a 6–5 favorite to win the rematch. At stake was Ali's NABF title.

"There wasn't the same atmosphere at the Garden as there was for the first fight," recalled Tom Kenville, who worked publicity for Madison Square Garden. "It

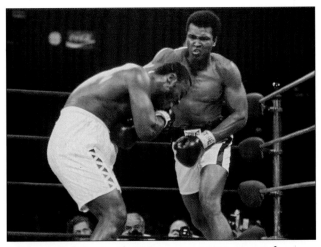

Ali beat Frazier in their January 1974 rematch, clearing the way for his title shot against George Foreman.

wasn't as big an event. There was no world title on the line. There was a sense that both of them had slipped a little."

"It was a tough fight," said Kenville. "All their fights were tough fights. Their styles dictated that. When those two got together, it was going to be a battle. Then there was the controversy and everyone was hollering and yelling. But you know, those things happen."

The first controversy came in the second round, when Ali wobbled Frazier with a straight right hand. Referee Tony Perez thought he heard the bell, so he separated the fighters. That gave Frazier extra time to recover. The other controversy stemmed from the Frazier camp. They complained that Perez allowed Ali to grab Frazier behind the neck and pull his head down repeatedly throughout the fight.

Those controversies overshadowed a very good heavyweight fight. While it was clearly not as exciting as their first or third bouts, Ali and Frazier fought hard for 12 rounds. There was more clinching and grabbing in this fight, but Ali hardly retreated to the ropes and scored the more impressive flurries. In this bout, when Frazier got too close, Ali decided not to slug with him. Instead, he tied him up in a clinch.

The end result was a close but clear unanimous decision for Ali. The scoring by rounds was 7–4–1, 8–4, and 6–5–1.

The only man left in the heavyweight division for Ali to fight was George Foreman—the man many boxing experts considered as the second coming of Sonny Liston.

The Rumble in the Jungle

In 1974, Ali met heavyweight champion George Foreman in Zaire, a country ruled by a ruthless dictator. The fight began at 4 A.M., with fans chanting, "Ali, kill him!"

Boxing is a sport for the young. The physical demands—speed, strength, and reflexes—make it difficult for an aging fighter to compete against both his opponent and Mother Nature.

While there have been a few ageless warriors who have succeeded, it seemed in the fall of 1974 that the era of Muhammad Ali was closing. The heavyweight division was in the firm grasp of a strong, young champion. Although Ali still competed on a world-class level, signs of his descent were evident.

Since returning from exile, Ali had been defeated by Joe Frazier and Ken Norton. Although he won rematches against both fighters, they were hardly convincing victories. At the age of 32, Ali's best fights seemed to reside in the past.

"Everybody kind of thought that Ali and Frazier would be relegated to the back of the line," said Madison Square Garden's boxing publicist, Tom Kenville. "George Foreman was the tiger of the future. Everybody felt that he would rule the heavyweight division for as long as he wanted to."

George Foreman had captured the heavyweight title in stunning fashion on January 22, 1973, when he knocked out Frazier in the second round. So devastating was Foreman's attack that he dropped Frazier six times in four and a half minutes.

Foreman was an imposing physical specimen. He stood 6'4", weighed a solid 220 pounds, and his quiet, brooding demeanor and fearsome power were reminiscent of Sonny Liston's. In his second title defense, Foreman starched Norton in two rounds. The two men who had defeated Ali failed to last a total of four rounds with the young champion.

That this fight happened is due largely to the efforts of promoter Don King, who at the time was a fringe player in the boxing world. King was able to persuade Foreman and Ali into competing by guaranteeing them each slightly more than $5 million in purse money. But while King had his fighters, he did not have the dollars. The promoter and his partners at a firm called Video Techniques began to shop the fight around the world. They found a willing ally in Mobutu Sese Seko, the president of Zaire, a country located in the heart of Central Africa. In 1965, Mobutu had assumed control of Zaire, formerly known as the Belgian Congo, and ruled the country with an iron fist until his regime was ousted in 1997.

Mobutu guaranteed $10 million in purse money and invested millions more in a stadium to host the fight, in telephone lines for the world media, and in electronic technology that would make it possible to broadcast the fight on closed-circuit television. Mobutu, who until his death in 1997 had been referred to as a homicidal dictator, said the fight was a gift to his people, but ultimately he hoped the publicity the bout generated would enhance the image of Zaire around the world.

King planned a three-day music festival before the bout that would include such African-American performing artists as James Brown, B.B. King, and the Pointer Sisters. King envisioned the entire promotion as a celebration of black culture. But when the promoter printed the slogan "From the Slave Ship to the Championship" on a fight poster, he was told to destroy them because they offended Zairians.

Ali quickly nicknamed the showdown "The Rumble in the Jungle." Once again, he was at his best when the cameras were rolling:

"George Foreman is nothing but a big mummy," said Ali. "I've officially named him "The Mummy." He moves like a slow mummy, and there ain't no mummy gonna whup the great Muhammad Ali."

"I think it would be fitting that I go out of boxing just like I came in, shocking the world by beating a big, bad, ugly monster that no one could beat."

Foreman, whose public persona today is that of an affable, grandfatherly slugger, was content to play the part of sullen champion. Ali's diatribes were hardly a distraction.

"This man has been talking since he started boxing," said Foreman at a televised press conference. "People have broken his jaw, knocked him out...one guy knocked his legs so far up in the air, I thought he

Ali's doctor, Ferdie Pacheco, said that Ali gained inner strength from being in Africa.

was gonna take off. And he got up and started talking. So there's no way I'm gonna be able to stop him from talking."

In hyping the fight, Ali promised he would dance around the ponderous champ. "I'm gonna float like a butterfly and sting like a bee; George can't hit what he can't see," he said. Ali even planned a special punch for Foreman. He called it "The Ghetto Whopper," naming it such because he said it was thrown in the ghetto at three o'clock in the morning. The correlation was that Ali and Foreman would fight at 3 A.M. in Zaire to accommodate American closed-circuit TV audiences.

With the bout scheduled for September 25, 1974, the fighters departed for Africa on September 10. Once in Zaire, Foreman led a reclusive existence, living in the Western-style Intercontinental Hotel in downtown Kinshasa. Ali stayed at a government compound in

N'Sele, approximately 40 miles outside of the city. Mobutu made good on his promise that the accommodations would be first-rate.

"Most of the writers stayed in N'Sele," said Dave Anderson, the *New York Times*'s Pulitzer Prize-winning sports columnist. "It was the place where they entertained diplomats when they came to Zaire. It was very nice. Ali also stayed in N'Sele in a big villa. It was like a house and it was about 30 yards from the Congo River. That was the fastest-flowing river I ever saw."

Ali immediately won over the citizens of Zaire, who repeatedly chanted, *"Ali, bomaye!"*—"Ali, kill him!"

"Almost from the beginning, Ali was embraced by the people in Zaire," said Bobby Goodman, who worked publicity for the Ali camp. "Muhammad had a reputation that he was a man fighting for his people. The Africans embraced that. George was this hulk-

Zaire President Mobutu Sese Seko greets Ali, with wife Belinda.

ing kind of guy who absolutely didn't have the personality Ali had, and he didn't have the bubbly personality he has today. Once Muhammad found out what *Ali, bomaye* meant, everywhere we went, he had the people chanting, '*Ali bomaye!*'"

Then, just eight days before the fight, disaster struck. Foreman was sparring with journeyman heavyweight Bill McMurray when he suffered a cut above his right eye.

"The training center was in N'Sele, and when Foreman got cut, I went over there right away," recalled Goodman. "Dick Sadler, who was Foreman's trainer, asked, 'What do you think?' I said I think we have a five- to six-week postponement. Then I started to hear sirens. Modunga Bula arrived; he was like the Henry Kissinger of Zaire. [He was an advisor to Mobutu.] Bula said, 'I hear there's a problem.' So I told him we'd have to postpone the fight five or six weeks. Bula looked at me and said, 'It's impossible. The fight will go on as scheduled.'"

Both camps were frustrated. Ali thought of several options—allowing Foreman to fight with headgear, flying in Joe Frazier to take Foreman's place, or even shifting the fight to the Unites States—but none of the options were feasible. Meanwhile, rumors were circulating that Mobutu would not allow the fighters to leave the country.

"We had an emergency meeting to take care of the postponement," said Goodman. "I told Bula, 'We'll be back in five weeks and the fight will go off as scheduled.' He said, 'No. No one leaves.'"

Ali and Foreman stayed in Zaire, but the bout was rescheduled for October 30 at 4 A.M. In an NBC special celebrating the fight, Dr. Ferdie Pacheco, Ali's physician, told how Ali spent his nights sitting by the Congo River. "More than anyone," recalled Pacheco, "Muhammad Ali seemed to draw power from the location, from Africa, that he was close to his roots."

> ## "I told Bula, 'We'll be back in five weeks and the fight will go off as scheduled.' He said, 'No. No one leaves.'"
> ### –Bobby Goodman, publicity man for the Ali camp

On fight night, the 26-year-old Foreman entered the *Stade du 20 Mai* (20th of May Stadium) a 5-1 betting favorite. He had scored 24 consecutive knockouts, the last eight coming in two rounds or less. But to the 60,000 fans in attendance, many of them chanting, "*Ali, bomaye,*" Foreman was the enemy.

"I thought that Foreman would win," said Anderson. "I remember going down to the dressing room area about two hours before the fight to see if both fighters had arrived. I was near Foreman's dressing room, and at the other end of the hall I saw Ali coming in and he looked huge. I thought to myself, maybe I picked the wrong guy."

At the opening bell, Ali raced across the ring. He landed the first punch of the fight, sending a clear message that he was not intimidated. Much to the delight of the crowd, Ali landed several sharp lead rights in the first round. Each right hand generated a roar from the crowd and made Foreman seem a little less invincible.

Then, midway through Round 2, Ali retreated to the ropes. It seemed like a disastrous idea because his entire strategy was based on movement. He was supposed to dance, stick, and move, and when Foreman was sufficiently tired, he would go for the kill. Standing along the ropes, Ali was merely a stationary target. That was where Foreman wanted the fight. And yet when Ali put his back to the ropes, Foreman almost looked as if he didn't know what to do.

There were moments when Foreman delivered brutal body shots to Ali's midsection. And occasionally he'd land a strong blow to Ali's head. Somehow, the 32-year-old Ali endured each punch. Eventually, Foreman was reduced to throwing wide, amateurish punches that landed on Ali's gloves or that Ali leaned away from. Ali used the loose ropes to avoid many punches.

Near the end of the third round, Ali sprung off the ropes with a quick combination. When Ali countered, Foreman appeared defenseless. Each time Ali punched, Foreman stopped throwing his own punches. Ali's speed was beginning to neutralize Foreman's power. Still, Ali's corner was concerned, and Dundee implored him round after round to stay off the ropes.

By the fifth round, Foreman's face began to swell. But the champion still pursued Ali, flailing away with blows to the arms, shoulders, gloves, and kidneys. Few of Foreman's punches reached their desired destination, but when they did Ali never appeared to be hurt. With 25 seconds left in that round, Ali again exploded off the ropes with a flurry, and both fighters swung freely at each other until the bell.

Ali opened the sixth round pumping his left jab as Foreman slowly lumbered after him. As the fight went

Ali looks on as referee Zack Clayton counts out George Foreman near the end of Round 8.

on, it was clear that Foreman was fatigued. After the seventh, Dundee remarked in the corner, "Foreman's sleepwalking."

Foreman had not seen the eighth round of a fight since 1971. When the bell rang to begin the eighth round in Zaire, Ali snapped Foreman's head back with a jab and right hand. Then he retreated to the ropes and Foreman walked after him, taking each step as if his feet were sinking into sand. Ali was inactive through much of the round. Then, with approximately 20 seconds left, Ali stunned him with a counter right. Another right sent Foreman lurching into the ropes. Ali moved out of the corner and Foreman followed. Then a quick right-left combination sent Foreman twisting to the canvas in the center of the ring. Referee Zack Clayton counted him out as the round came to an end.

Ali had shocked the world again.

"I don't think people give Ali enough credit for the Foreman fight," said George Chuvalo, the tough heavyweight contender who fought both Ali and Foreman. "He relied on his brains in that fight. He counterpunched. He fought the perfect fight."

In the aftermath of the Rumble in the Jungle, President Gerald Ford invited Ali to the White House. He was named Fighter of the Year by the Boxing Writers Association of America and Sportsman of the Year by *Sports Illustrated*. Fans relived the fight 22 years later in the film *When We Were Kings*, which won an Oscar for best documentary.

Immediately after the fight, David Frost attempted to interview Ali for the closed-circuit television audience. Ali quickly took control and quieted his joyous dressing room. "Everybody stop talking right now. Attention," Ali said. Then he focused his gaze directly at the camera. His right eye was slightly swollen and discolored. He pointed his right index finger at the camera and began to lecture. "I told you, all of my critics, I told you that I was the greatest of all time when I beat Sonny Liston. I told you today I'm still the greatest of all time...Never again say that I'm going to be defeated. Never again make me the underdog until I'm about 50 years old. Then you might get me."

Ali became only the second man in history to regain the heavyweight title. He was suddenly young again.

The Thrilla in Manila

*On October 1, 1975, Ali and Joe Frazier,
two aging warriors, met in 100-degree heat in
the Philippines. After 14 rounds, the battered
fighters could barely get off their stools.*

There are few rivalries in the world of sports that can match the one between Muhammad Ali and Joe Frazier. It was a rivalry fueled by the intense competitive spirit that burned inside each man. Ali and "Smokin' Joe" delivered three compelling and classic battles that defined the decade of the 1970s.

When they met for the third time, on October 1, 1975, in Manila, Philippines, they engaged in a fight that is now regarded as one of the greatest in boxing history. They took center stage before the world, with the grandest title in all of sports at stake, and defined what it was to fight with heart and courage.

"Their styles were just meant for each other," said Ali's trainer, Angelo Dundee. "It is remarkable. No matter where or when they fought, if you put them together you couldn't have a bad fight. I think they both brought each other to a higher level. They brought the best out of each other."

George Benton, a top middleweight from the 1960s who worked Frazier's corner for the third Ali fight, considers the "Thrilla in Manila" the greatest title fight in the history of the heavyweight division. "These were two warriors in the ring," marveled Benton, who later trained heavyweight champions Leon Spinks and Oliver McCall. "Joe was so determined. He made it very, very difficult for Ali. But you can't take nothing away from Ali. He was determined, too."

The fight wound up in Manila because the president of the Philippines, Ferdinand Marcos, promised to bankroll the event. Marcos had political motives for staging the fight, hoping that he would gain popularity among his constituents by bringing the world's most famous athlete to the Philippines. He was right.

Ali was beloved around the globe, and when the fight with Frazier was announced, the master showman put his act into high gear. At the press conference, though, Ali took the prefight hype to yet another undesirable level. Today, his actions would be cause for condemnation. But at the time, the media adored Ali and his antics. Seated at a table were Ali, promoter Don King, and Frazier. Standing behind them, smoking a cigar, was legendary sports artist LeRoy Neiman. Once the cameras started rolling, Ali began to perform.

"It's gonna be a thrilla and a chilla and a killa when I get the gorilla in Manila," shouted Ali.

Frazier was smiling, but he found nothing funny about Ali. Then it got worse. Ali pulled out a small rubber gorilla and said to Frazier, "I got your conscience with me, and I'm gonna keep it right here in my pocket." Ali placed the gorilla in his breast pocket.

Remarkably, Frazier remained composed and dignified. He said simply, "It's kind of nice to know that it's only about two or three months away and I'll be the champ again."

Yet throughout the buildup to the fight, Frazier would endure the ugly taunts of Ali. It seemed each time a camera was rolling, Ali would display the gorilla and, while holding it in his left hand, punch it repeatedly with his right. All the while, he'd be shouting, "Come on gorilla, we in Manila. Come on gorilla, this is a thrilla."

> ## "It's gonna be a thrilla and a chilla and a killa when I get the gorilla in Manila."
> ### —Ali

Ali believed that Frazier was over the hill. The challenger had been knocked out by George Foreman in 1973 and had lost on points to Ali in 1974. There was nothing to convince Ali that he would be in a competitive fight. So confident was the champion that he brought his mistress, Veronica Porsche, to Manila as part of his entourage. It was kept relatively quiet until Ali brought her to meet President Marcos, and they posed for photos with the first family of the Philippines. When those photos were published in America, Ali's wife, Belinda, departed for Manila and ended their marriage. Still, as the fight approached, the champion was unfazed by the controversy.

Frazier never appreciated Ali's hijinks. His bitterness turned to hatred by the time of their third fight, which was promoted by Don King (center).

To accommodate closed-circuit TV back in the United States, the bout was scheduled to begin at 10:45 A.M. Manila time. Ali entered the ring a 2–1 favorite. He was 33 years old and weighed 224½ pounds. Frazier was 31 years old and weighed 215½ pounds.

They fought in the Philippine Coliseum, which was actually located in Quezon City, six miles outside of Manila. There were 28,000 people in attendance, including President Marcos and the first lady, Imelda. There have been various reports concerning the temperature inside the arena. It has been reported by different sources to have ranged anywhere from 95 to 110 degrees. The humidity was oppressive and, once the arena was filled with people, the air conditioning was useless. It was as if they were fighting in a sauna.

"Manila was hotter than the fight in Zaire with George Foreman," recalled Dundee. "There was a tin roof overhead, and that accentuated the heat. Plus, there were all the TV lights and the air wasn't circulating."

Despite the conditions, Ali was upbeat as he entered the ring. He was convinced that Frazier was past his prime and continued his frivolous approach to the fight. A huge trophy sat in the center of the ring, and Ali picked it up during the introductions and brought it back to his corner. Then, when he heard a smattering of boos, he acted as if he were crying.

When the bell rang, Ali started fast, determined to knock Frazier out. Rather than dance, he stood flat-footed in the center of the ring and blitzed the challenger with combinations. There is a belief in boxing that the best fights are those between great fighters who are slightly past their prime. The reasoning is that they retain the same warrior's spirit, but lose a notch in speed and reflexes. The result is a bout in which a lot of punches land. In retrospect, that was clearly the case in Manila. Ali and Frazier were not as sharp or fast as they were in 1971, but both fighters were still equipped with ample courage.

Ali continued to pepper Frazier with punches throughout the first four rounds, even wobbling him on several occasions. In the fifth round, however, Ali began to slow down. He abandoned his fast-paced attack and was content to fight with his back on the ropes. The shift in pace rejuvenated the challenger. He began driving his vaunted hook into Ali's body. For the first time, Frazier was fighting with confidence, and the crowd energized him further with chants of "Frazier, Frazier!"

During the round, commentator Don Dunphy said to broadcast partner Flip Wilson, "Flip, it looks to me

as though this is going to be decided on conditioning."
He was correct. The sixth round opened with Frazier
driving Ali to the ropes with a pair of left hooks. Ali
countered sharply with two hooks of his own and dis-
lodged Frazier's mouthpiece. Undeterred, Frazier continued to bury punches into Ali's midsection, grunting
loudly with each blow. As the round ended, Ali slowly
walked back to his corner, a look of disgust on his
face. He had come upon the realization that he was
in a fight.

In the first minute of Round 8, the fighters engaged
in a vicious multipunch exchange that neither man
backed off from. Frazier closed the round strong, again
pinning Ali to the ropes and alternating his hook
between the body and head. The suffocating humidity and the nonstop punching were taking their toll on
each fighter. The Thrilla in Manila had become a battle of wills. This contest would no longer be determined by skill, but by determination.

"With the intensity of the fight and the heat, I was
concerned about Muhammad," recalled Dundee. "But
I felt Muhammad was winning the fight. I don't know
how they did it. To fight the way they fought under
those conditions is remarkable. But nothing surprises
me with fighters. Just to be a fighter you have to be
special. Not a world champion, not a contender, just
a fighter. They're a different breed. And nothing has
ever surprised me with Muhammad."

It was no surprise, then, that after absorbing a terrible beating in the 11th round, Ali began to march
back into the fight. Somehow, the champion emerged
from his stool energized for the 12th round. He began
pumping rapid combinations at Frazier, who was
bleeding from the mouth and losing his vision due to

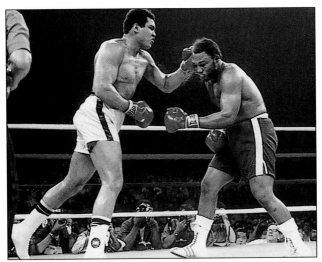

Despite insufferable heat and humidity, the great warriors punched and counterpunched relentlessly for 14 rounds.

the swelling around his eyes. Early in Round 13, a right cross by Ali sent Frazier's mouthpiece flying across the ring and into the press section. Ali continued to punch in combination as Frazier continued to plod after him. Chants of "Ali, Ali, Ali" began to rise from the arena. A right-left combination caused Frazier to stumble backward. Somehow, though, with his eyes reduced to slits, he remained on his feet. Frazier was no longer employing his customary bob-and-weave attack. He was standing erect, accepting all of Ali's punishment.

The 14th round was dominated by Ali. He began to back Frazier up with left-right combinations. At one point, Frazier was pinned to the ropes under the relentless pressure of Ali's punches. Somehow, he again survived the round. Both men walked grimly back to their corners, referee Carlos Padilla aiding Frazier. When Ali returned to his corner, he instructed Dundee, "Cut 'em off." Ali was referring to his gloves, a sign that he was ready to submit. Dundee ignored him and began to prepare him for the final round.

The 15th round would never start. The fighting was over. There would be no decisive blow or stunning knockout. The most brutal fight in heavyweight history would end with an act of humanity by one of boxing's elder statesman—Eddie Futch.

"I thought Ali was getting ready to quit," recalled Benton. "Dundee talked him out of it, and then he looked over to our corner and saw that the fight might get stopped."

> ## "Sit down, son. It's all over. No one will ever forget what you did here today."
> ### –Eddie Futch to Joe Frazier after the 14th round

As Dundee worked on Ali, Futch had already decided to stop the fight. The scene in that corner is one of the most dramatic in boxing history. Frazier, his eyes nearly closed, his mouth bloodied, rose from his stool to protest as Futch summoned Padilla to the corner. "But I want him, boss," Frazier said to Futch. Futch then touched Frazier on the shoulder. The words that followed are legendary. "Sit down, son," Futch told the warrior. "It's all over. No one will ever forget what you did here today."

That moment remains one of the most difficult of Futch's career. But he has no regrets about his decision. "Joe's vision was impaired to the point that he couldn't avoid Ali's punches," said Futch. "He couldn't see them coming. I wasn't going to allow him to take any more punches. Joe was getting hit with so many punches. And all it takes is one to cause some permanent damage."

Benton echoed Futch's sentiments. "It's always difficult to stop a fight when your guy is going good," he said. "But you always have to think about the fighter. It's better to come out of a fight with two eyes than to come out blind. It had gotten to the point where it was just too much."

When the fight ended, Ali collapsed in his corner. Moments later, he was helped onto his stool by his cornermen, who frantically waved towels in his face in an attempt to revive him.

The competitiveness of the fight was not reflected in the official scoring. At the time of the stoppage, Ali led on all three scorecards: 8–5–1, 8–2–4, and 9–3–2. It was indeed a much closer fight.

"It was like death," Ali said after the fight. "The closest thing to dyin' that I know of."

For a moment after the fight, Frazier stopped hating Ali and praised the champion. "Man, I hit him with punches that'd bring down the walls of a city," he told *Sports Illustrated*. "Lawdy, lawdy, he's a great champion."

They were both great champions. The fight was named "Fight of the Year" by *The Ring* magazine, and Ali earned "Fighter of the Year" honors from *The Ring*. In an unprecedented move, the Boxing Writers Association of America named both Ali and Frazier the

"Fighter of the Year." Futch was only half correct. No one will ever forget what Frazier *and* Ali did in Manila on October 1, 1975.

Afterward, as he had done before, Ali hinted at retirement. "I'm tired of being the whole game," he said at a press conference. "Let the other guys do the fighting. You might never see Ali in the ring again."

Ali, and Frazier as well, would never fight at such a high level again. They had each left a piece of themselves—a portion of their fighting hearts—in that ring in Manila. Unfortunately, they would both return to the ring.

Jabbing with Cosell

Howard Cosell, the cerebral lawyer turned broadcaster, played straight man for Ali, inspiring nonstop animated banter from the champ. They were, said Cosell, "an inseparable television team."

Howard Cosell became as big a part of American culture as the sports and the athletes he covered. Cosell's presence at a sporting event was a clear indication that the event was indeed special. Cosell's immense success and stature in the broadcast industry can be traced directly back to Muhammad Ali.

"We would be locked in the public's mind as an inseparable television team," wrote Cosell in his book, *I Never Played the Game.* That may be a bit of an overstatement from Cosell, whose expansive vocabulary was matched in size only by his enormous ego. But the fighter and the broadcaster were indeed quite a twosome. Cosell was the perfect straight man for the charismatic Ali.

The relationship between Ali and Cosell was like none other between an athlete and a member of the media. Observers of the media say that Ali made Cosell, and that is probably an accurate assessment. However, Cosell did a pretty fair job of providing Ali with plenty of exposure. But considering Ali's immense appeal, it was hardly a difficult assignment. Ali possessed what few fighters are blessed with—crossover appeal. That means he was an attraction to the casual sports fan and not just the boxing fan. Since the end of boxing's Golden Age, only a handful of fighters can boast of this—Ali, Sugar Ray Leonard, Roberto Duran, and Mike Tyson.

In Thomas Hauser's book, *Muhammad Ali: His Life and Times*, Cosell said, "Muhammad Ali is a figure

The mutual respect and admiration the two men felt for each other continued well after they had retired.

transcendental to sport....The only other person to come out of sports who might be as important as Ali was Jackie Roosevelt Robinson."

Cosell assumed the mythical title as the voice of boxing from Don Dunphy. While Dunphy still did his share of major fights on closed-circuit TV through the 1970s, Cosell was broadcasting boxing to millions of fans each weekend on ABC. Cosell was a witness to Ali's greatest triumphs and tragedies. He did color commentary on the radio broadcast when Ali first won the heavyweight title from Sonny Liston, and he called the second Leon Spinks fight when Ali captured the title for the third time. Conversely, he remained by Ali's side when he was exiled from boxing, and he was ringside when Ali failed to regain the title from former sparring partner Larry Holmes.

Cosell: You seem awfully truculent today, champ.

Ali: I don't know what truculent means, but if it's good, that's me.

Cosell displayed uncommon integrity and loyalty when he supported Ali through the champ's exile. Cosell covered Ali's draft induction, and he lambasted the government and state athletic commissions when Ali was stripped of his title. He also criticized the sports media for sitting idly by as it happened. If Ali were no longer the champion in the ring, Cosell would champion his cause away from the ring. During that period, Cosell was worried about his job at ABC because the stance he was taking was unpopular with mainstream America. But that stance would earn him a friend for life. Here was a typical Cosell tirade on Ali's exile: Of the sportswriters who supported Ali's banishment, he simply called them "...a disgrace to the journalism they pretend to be a part of."

The egotistic Cosell once said: "The single fulcrum that projected me into national prominence was *Monday Night Football*—three hours in prime time. Bill Cosby doesn't get it, Carson doesn't get it, Lucy doesn't get it, Rowan and Martin don't get it. We get three hours in prime time. And don't tell me it's not entertainment."

Cosell was indeed good entertainment. Cosell and Ali, however, were extraordinary. Perhaps their best exchange took place prior to Ali's fight with Zora Folley in 1967. Ali was uncharacteristically sullen during the course of the interview, which prompted Cosell to remark: "You seem awfully truculent today, champ." Ali responded: "I don't know what truculent means, but if it's good, that's me."

In 1974, Cosell found himself as the man in the middle when Ali and Frazier nearly came to blows in ABC's television studio five days before their rematch. Frazier was initially going to pass on the appearance because he felt, quite correctly, that Ali would use the show as a public forum to insult him. Cosell guaranteed Frazier that would not happen and that he would personally restrict the comments to boxing. During the course of the show, it was Frazier who broke the truce when he made a reference to Ali going to the hospital after their first fight. While Cosell tried to keep the peace, Ali could not help himself and responded by calling Frazier ignorant. Frazier rose from his chair and confronted Ali. Things appeared to be getting out of control when Ali's brother, Rahaman, stepped onto the stage. But just before anything severe could happen, Ali grabbed Frazier in a bear hug and the two wrestled each other to the floor. The fighters were separated moments later, and the rematch eventually took place in the ring.

After Ali defeated George Foreman to regain the heavyweight title later in 1974, he boasted that he would like to fight Frazier and Foreman in the same night. He spoke about taking the fight to Russia or China because it would be illegal in the United States. He ended the monologue by saying he would jump over the ring's ropes and pull the toupee off Cosell's head.

Cosell's toupee was a constant Ali target. Some times, during interviews, he'd mockingly raise his hand as if he were going to swipe at the toupee. Another time, before his fight with Jimmy Young, Ali was speaking to a group of students at the University of Maryland and offered to pay anyone $1,000 if they could bring him Cosell's toupee.

In the documentary *Howard Cosell at Large: What Is He Really Like?*, the cameras caught Ali and Cosell at their best. A group of teenagers in New York City's Central Park circled around Ali and Cosell, and Ali started to perform. He asked the kids if he should slap Cosell for asking irritating questions, and the smiling teenagers applauded.

"I've taken enough of you," said Ali in mock anger. "You can't fight. You can't throw no punches. You don't have no muscles. You never had a physical confrontation.... And you are gonna stand up here and tell me about my legs and about football? You don't know about everything."

Suddenly, Ali placed his fist beneath Cosell's jaw as Cosell tried his best to suppress his laughter. "Well, I'm getting sick and tired," continued Ali. "I'm gonna tell the world there really ain't nothing to you." To which Cosell dead-panned: "Don't touch me. I'll beat your brains out."

By the late 1970s, Cosell grew disenchanted with the sport of boxing. The first reason was Don King's scandalous U.S. Boxing Championship Tournament. The tournament was televised by ABC until it was revealed that some fighters gained entry to the tournament by using falsified records or by paying kickbacks. Even Ali could not escape Cosell's wrath. When the champion defended his title against Alfredo Evangelista in '77, Cosell labeled the bout dull and wondered aloud before his television audience how Evangelista was maneuvered into a shot for the heavyweight title.

Then Cosell broadcast the 1982 heavyweight title fight between champion Larry Holmes and challenger Randall "Tex" Cobb. The fight was a gross mismatch, and Cosell repeatedly called for it to be stopped during the broadcast. He said the fight was an advertisement for the abolishment of boxing. After that fight, Cosell vowed never again to broadcast a professional fight. He kept his promise, restricting his boxing work to the Olympics.

As time passed, Cosell was protective of Ali's mystique, even if it meant a dose of tough love. By 1984, it was clear that Ali's health was slipping and his public image was suffering. At the Summer Olympics that year in Los Angeles, where Cosell was broadcasting boxing matches, longtime Ali photographer Howard Bingham asked Cosell to interview Ali on the air. He

Ali uses Cosell as a prop during a light-hearted moment at his weigh-in against Chuck Wepner (right).

refused because he felt Ali would embarrass himself. Later that year, when Ali was diagnosed with Parkinson's syndrome, ABC gained access to the former champ in the hospital. The network asked Cosell to interview Ali for the news program *Nightline*. Again he refused. "That isn't journalism," Cosell said in his book, "that's exploitation."

Cosell died of cancer in 1995.

The World's Champion

Ali fought all over the globe, including Ireland, Indonesia, Japan, and Malaysia. In the 1970s, he became one of the most recognizable people on earth.

M uhammad Ali truly defined the term world champion. His title fights were global events because he was willing to fight anywhere in the world. He brought the heavyweight championship to third-world countries and made faraway cities like Kuala Lumpur and Kinshasa famous. Of course, the countries Ali fought in often guaranteed him a substantial purse, but it was usually worth the investment.

Ali fought in 12 foreign countries—Great Britain (three times), Canada (twice), Germany (twice), Japan, Switzerland, Ireland, Indonesia, Zaire, Malaysia, the Philippines, Puerto Rico, and the Bahamas—and on three different continents. He also embarked on exhibition tours that brought him to Scotland, Venezuela, and Argentina. At home in the United States, Ali fought in 12 different states and boxed exhibitions in three more.

While Floyd Patterson defended the heavyweight title in Toronto in 1961, one has to go back to the title reigns of John L. Sullivan (1885–1892) and Jack Johnson (1908–1915) to find another heavyweight champion who defended the throne outside of the United States.

In 1966, Ali experienced a controversy that forced him to fight outside the United States. His scheduled title fight against Ernie Terrell was moved from Chicago to Toronto due to Ali's stance on the draft. When the bout was moved, Terrell pulled out and rugged Canadian contender George Chuvalo was the replacement.

"Ali was loved in Toronto," said Chuvalo. "My hometown fans still loved me, but they appreciated Ali. It was like two favorites in the ring. It was good-will all around."

Ali was greeted with the same reception wherever he traveled. Bobby Goodman, Ali's publicist for much of the 1970s, estimated that he visited nearly 30 countries with the three-time heavyweight champ.

"Ali was not only the most recognizable boxer around the world, he was the most recognizable human being, period," said Goodman. "It was incredible when you saw the impact he had on people—the mere frenzy he caused just by his presence. It happened anywhere we went—Malaysia, the Philippines, Africa, Germany. And often we were dealing with heads of state, presidents, kings. It was such an incredible experience."

Between his epic fights in Zaire and Manila, Ali defended the title three times in the span of 100 days.

The first defense of his second reign as heavyweight champion came against veteran contender Chuck Wepner in Cleveland on March 24, 1975. Wepner was a rugged fighter from Bayonne, New Jersey, who had a tendency to cut during fights.

"I caught Ali in the middle of his career," said Wepner. "He was 32 years old. If I had fought him in his prime, it would have been a much tougher fight for me. He was a great fighter. But remember, I was 38. He caught me near the end, too."

Wepner's blood-and-guts style of boxing was Sylvester Stallone's inspiration when he wrote the first *Rocky* screenplay. The highlight of Wepner's night came in the ninth round when he floored Ali with a right hand to the chest. Wepner became only the fourth man—Sonny Banks, Henry Cooper, and Joe Frazier were the others—to send Ali to the canvas. Ali later claimed that Wepner stepped on his foot, causing him to lose his balance.

The fight ended when referee Tony Perez stopped it in the 15th and final round. Ali was ahead on the scorecards, but the stoppage hurt the courageous Wepner more than any punch Ali landed.

"Sure that stills bothers me," said Wepner. "It was the only time I was ever down or off my feet in my career. The referee said my eyes were glassy or that I was incoherent. But I knew where I was. I answered his questions. He said, 'Where are you?' I said, 'Cleveland.' Ali wasn't going to knock me out. The thing was that I was completely exhausted. It's because I didn't stop coming; that's the way I fought. I wish they would have let it go."

Less than two months later, on May 16, Ali took on hard-punching contender Ron Lyle in Las Vegas. Once

No champion before or since has fought in as many different countries as Ali, seen here outpointing Joe Bugner in Malaysia in July 1975.

again, he employed the Rope-a-Dope. Lyle didn't go for it. Instead, he stood in the middle of the ring, beckoning Ali to come and fight. Ali appeared a little bored and a little frustrated, and the scorecards reflected as much. After 10 rounds, Lyle led on two scorecards and the third was even. Then Ali exploded with a furious barrage of punches in the 11th, forcing referee Ferd Hernandez to stop the fight.

On July 1, Ali traveled halfway around the world for a rematch with Joe Bugner. The locale was Kuala Lumpur, Malaysia. Ali picked Malaysia for two reasons: He was guaranteed a $2 million purse and he would be fighting in a Muslim country. The fight itself was uneventful, and Ali easily outpointed Bugner over 15 rounds.

From Malaysia, Ali's next stop was the Philippines, where he conquered Joe Frazier in the classic "Thrilla

No other athlete has ever been celebrated by as many world leaders as has Ali, seen here with India Prime Minister Indira Gandhi.

in Manila" on October 1, 1975. At this point of his career, Ali flirted with retirement, and in retrospect it would have been the perfect time to step down from the throne. But Muhammad resumed his incredible pace of activity.

Ali returned to the ring less than five months after the Thrilla in Manila and knocked out the unheralded Jean Pierre Coopman in five rounds on February 20, 1976, in San Juan, Puerto Rico. Two months later, he was back in the United States defending his title against Jimmy Young in Landover, Maryland.

The Young fight was a debacle for Ali. The crafty contender out of Philadelphia was a marginal talent. Like Coopman, he was expected to be another easy opponent. Ali approached the fight casually and weighed in at a career-high 230 pounds. Young was a reluctant warrior, fighting in spurts throughout 15 tedious rounds. There were times when he was quicker and sharper than Ali, but on six occasions over the course of the fight, he stuck his head between the ropes to escape Ali's attack. The result was a dreadfully boring 15-round decision win for Ali.

"Jimmy Young was purposely sticking his head out of the ropes to cause the referee to call time," said Goodman. "He just wanted to survive, and Jimmy Young was one of the all-time great survivors. I don't think he won the fight. Ali didn't really overtrain for the fight. I mean, he knew Young couldn't hurt him. In Ali's mind, it was hard to get up for a fight like that."

Three months later, Ali somewhat redeemed himself by knocking out Englishman Richard Dunn in five rounds in a bout held in Munich, Germany. However, his public image suffered another blow a month later when he engaged in a dreadfully dull 15-round exhibition against wrestling champion Antonio Inoki in Japan.

It was time for Ali to get serious again, and the opponent would be his old rival Ken Norton. The third Ali-Norton fight took place on September 28, 1976, at Yankee Stadium. In its 75-year history, Yankee Stadium has played host to 30 world-title fights. Among the most historic boxing moments inside the "House that Ruth Built" were the second Joe Louis-Max

Schmeling fight, Sugar Ray Robinson vs. Joey Maxim, and the third Willie Pep-Sandy Saddler bout.

"It was a very big fight," said Arthur Mercante, who refereed the Ali-Norton fight. "Not only was it exciting because it was their third meeting and it was held in Yankee Stadium, but the question on everyone's mind was, 'Could Norton do it again?'"

Ali and Norton had split their first two fights. Each was decided in the last round. The third fight figured to be the same type of chess match. This time, Ali added another element—psychological warfare. It started at the weigh-in.

We sang 'Take Norton Out at the Ballpark' to the tune of 'Take Me Out to the Ballgame.' Angelo [Dundee] had us rehearsing that."
—Tom Kenville, publicity man for Ali's camp

"Ali let a black cat out of a bag at the weigh-in, and Norton freaked out," recalled Tom Kenville, who was in charge of publicity for Ali's camp. "We had signs that read Norton makes dirty pictures because he appeared in the movie *Mandingo*. We sang 'Take Norton Out at the Ballpark' to the tune of 'Take Me Out to the Ballgame.' Angelo [Dundee] had us rehearsing that."

The buildup was palpable in New York City, as 30,289 attended the fight. It's difficult to assess how many were paying customers. With the New York City police on strike, hundreds of fans crashed the gates.

In fact, Mercante's son James, who was then a midshipman at the U.S. Merchant Marine Academy, arrived in uniform to watch the fights with several cadets, and they were pressed into service as security guards. It was a heavyweight title fight at a major New York stadium. There was a time when that was the norm, but in 1976 it could very well have been the last chance to see Ali fight, or to attend a fight at Yankee Stadium. Or both.

"I was aware of the history Yankee Stadium has played in boxing," said Mercante. "I was there the night Joey Maxim fought Sugar Ray Robinson. The heat was awful. I believe it was the hottest night ever for a fight. They had to replace [referee] Ruby Goldstein in the 10th round with Ray Miller. But the weather wasn't a factor for the Ali-Norton fight."

The conditions and atmosphere meant nothing to Norton. He was focused simply on defeating Ali.

"I was so pumped up for the third fight that it could have been snowing or hailing and I wouldn't have felt a thing," said Norton. "I did roadwork outside and I boxed outside, so my body was already acclimated to the weather. I was in top condition. My mind was totally on the fight. My mind was on Ali. When you fight Ali, you couldn't think about anything else or you'd get spanked. You had to bring yourself to another level. You had to bring yourself to Ali's level—mentally and physically."

Norton stormed to an early lead in the fight. His awkward style, quick jab, and effective defense gave Ali trouble in all three of their fights. After eight rounds, Norton led on the scorecards, 5–3 (twice) and 6–2.

Ali's reign as king of the heavyweights appeared to be closing. Somehow, at the age of 34, he pulled out another miracle. Ali tapped into his seemingly bottomless reservoir of courage and began dancing, jabbing, and outhustling the younger and stronger Norton.

Once again, as in their first two fights, the final round would decide the outcome of the contest. Norton's manager, confident of victory, advised his fighter to simply survive the round. That was the difference. Norton came out to survive—and Ali came out to win. Despite a surge by Norton in the final 30 seconds, Ali captured the 15th round and was awarded a close unanimous decision. The scoring by rounds was 8–7 (twice) and 8–6–1. There hasn't been a professional boxing match at Yankee Stadium since.

Ali, renowned for his altruism, plays with children at a hospital in England after donating a bus to the facility in 1977.

"It was very difficult to rebound from the third fight," said Norton. "In fact, I never did. My concentration on boxing went into a tailspin after that."

Ali's career, though, didn't skip a beat.

After an eight-month rest, long by Ali's standards, the champion returned to the ring on May 16, 1977, and scored a 15-round unanimous decision over Alfredo Evangelista in Landover, Maryland. He was then back in action again on September 29 against the hard-hitting Earnie Shavers.

The Shavers bout took place at Madison Square Garden, and Shavers rattled Ali repeatedly throughout the fight. Shavers, though, was never able to finish the job. When in trouble, Ali either covered up or smothered his opponent. When he had room to box, Ali outslicked his one-dimensional opponent. The heavy-handed Shavers may have inflicted more damage, but Ali scored more points. The scoring by the three judges was 9–6 (twice) and 9–5–1 in favor of the champion. Once again, he came away with another close unanimous decision.

It was becoming painfully clear that Ali was slipping.

The Spinks Jinx

On February 15, 1978, Leon Spinks—the gap-toothed Olympic champion—upset the great Ali. In the rematch, Muhammad fought for an unprecedented third world title.

Leon Spinks was just 10 years old when Muhammad Ali upset Sonny Liston to win the heavyweight title in 1964. At the time, Spinks was busy navigating life through a tough East St. Louis ghetto, never dreaming that one day he might meet his idol inside a boxing ring.

Spinks later enlisted in the United States Marine Corps and began a storied amateur boxing career that would include three consecutive national titles (1974–76) in the light-heavyweight division. Ali himself had won the same titles in 1959 and 1960.

Spinks would take another step down the trail blazed by Ali when he made the 1976 U.S. Olympic team. Spinks was a member of one of the most decorated Olympic teams in history, and, like Ali in 1960, he captured a gold medal in the light-heavyweight division. Teammates Leo Randolph (flyweight), Howard Davis (lightweight), Sugar Ray Leonard (junior welterweight), and Leon's brother, Michael (middleweight), also won gold medals at the '76 games. Charles Mooney (bantamweight) captured a silver, while John Tate (heavyweight) took home a bronze medal.

The success of the '76 Olympians rejuvenated the sport of boxing in the United States. The Olympians turned pro with unprecedented fanfare, since boxing fans were anxious to watch their pro careers unfold. Spinks made his debut on January 15, 1977, and scored a fifth-round knockout over Bobby Smith.

Still, the idea of challenging Ali had not even entered his mind. But to Butch Lewis, Spinks's advisor and the man who brought him to promoter Bob Arum, it seemed like a great idea. Initially, Lewis's attempts to make such a match were rebuffed by Ali and his manager, Herbert Muhammad.

After his debut, Spinks scored four more knockouts before meeting Scott LeDoux, a legitimate main-event fighter, in a nationally televised bout. That bout ended in a 10-round draw, but Ali had watched it on television and suddenly the champ's interest was piqued. Negotiations for the Olympic hero to meet Ali were under way, but Spinks would first have to defeat a rated fighter before challenging for the title. Lewis's solution was to match Spinks with Italian heavyweight Alfio Righetti, who was rated by the WBC. While Righetti had an impressive numerical record (27–0), he had never fought outside of Italy. Spinks earned a 10-round decision over Righetti in November 1977, in Las Vegas to secure his title fight.

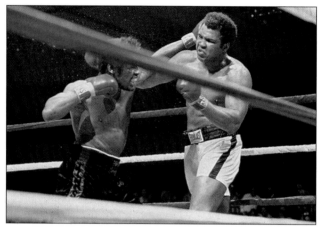

Ali was undertrained and unprepared when he fought Leon Spinks in February 1978.

Spinks entered the Ali fight with a record of 6–0–1 with five knockouts. Ali's record was 55–2 with 37 knockouts. The last man to challenge for the title with such sparse experience was Pete Rademacher. In 1956, Rademacher had captured the heavyweight gold medal at the Summer Olympics and immediately issued a challenge to heavyweight champion Floyd Patterson. The champ accepted, and Rademacher made his pro debut in a heavyweight title fight. Rademacher actually floored Patterson in Round 2, but the Olympic champ was knocked down seven times en route to a sixth-round knockout.

It seemed the same fate awaited Spinks.

Ali opened training camp at a bloated 242 pounds and weighed in for the fight at 224½. Spinks weighed 197¼. Uncharacteristically, Ali took a vow of silence before the fight and did not speak to reporters. But the gap-toothed challenger was already becoming a personality the press could enjoy. The question Spinks was most often asked was his thoughts on fighting a legend.

"Hey, what is there to think about?" Spinks told *Sports Illustrated*. "I've been fighting for my life since I was 10, so why is this fight different?"

The fight took place on February 15, 1978, at the Las Vegas Hilton. When the combatants walked into the ring, Ali was an 8–1 favorite.

"It was a surprisingly good fight," said Nigel Collins, then a Philadelphia-based writer for *The Ring* magazine and now that publication's editor-in-chief. "You had an over-the-hill, out-of-shape legend against a guy who just won the Olympics. I don't think much was expected. That it was such a competitive fight was a pleasant surprise."

No one, including Ali, expected much from Spinks. The champion gave away the early rounds of the fight, clowning and posturing with his young opponent. But Spinks fought hard from the opening bell. When Ali retreated to the ropes for the Rope-a-Dope, Spinks never slowed his attack. He may have been crude and awkward to watch, but Spinks was not intimidated and was in condition to fight for every second of the 15 rounds.

"You knew Leon would come to fight, and with a guy like that you always walk into the ring with confidence," said trainer George Benton, who worked with Spinks for the two Ali fights.

Lewis added Benton to the Spinks camp for two reasons. First, he respected Benton's cerebral approach to fighting and hoped the former middleweight contender could impart important knowledge to Spinks.

Lewis also knew that Benton was a disciple of Eddie Futch, who had helped Joe Frazier and Ken Norton defeat Ali.

Benton's game plan was simple. He told Spinks to "just hit him, just keep throwing punches." That was exactly what Spinks did. He hit Ali on the arms, the shoulders, the ribs, the hips...anywhere he could land a punch. The constant pressure of Spinks's punches prevented Ali from finding his own rhythm. It also took a toll on the champ's 36-year-old body.

In the 10th round, Ali sensed that his title was slipping away. He opened the round with a rally and backed Spinks up for the first time in the fight. He had Spinks trapped along the ropes, and a stiff right hand seemed to rock the challenger. But Spinks dug deep into his reservoir of determination and quickly shifted the momentum with a two-fisted flurry.

Sam Solomon, one of Spinks's trainers, knew what Ali had just found out. "As tough as Spinks is," Solomon said in *Sports Illustrated*, "he's even more dangerous when he's hurt."

By the 11th round, Ali had abandoned the Rope-a-Dope and waited for Spinks to tire. It never happened. The only one tiring was Ali. Still, he pressed on, fighting with the grim courage that made him a true champion. Although he was outgunned, Ali often stood toe-to-toe with Spinks in the 11th and 12th rounds.

Spinks regained command of the fight in the 14th round with a punishing body attack. As the 15th and final round started, Ali tried desperately to save his crown, staggering the challenger with a right hand. But it was Spinks who was stronger at the finish, closing with a clubbing right hand that landed at the bell.

Judges Lou Tabat and Harold Buck had the fight for Spinks, scoring it 145–140 and 144–141, respectively. Judge Art Lurie had it 143–142 for Ali. When it was over, Spinks still held his idol in high esteem. "He's still the greatest," the new champion told reporters. "I'm just the latest."

Fourteen years to the month after he "shook up the world" by beating Sonny Liston, Ali again shocked the sports world, by losing to Spinks.

Based on Ali's performance, the decision was not shocking—though the reality of the outcome was alarming. Leon Spinks had shocked the world, and Ali finally found out what it meant to be on the wrong side of his favorite expression. Someone in Ali's dressing room shouted "robbery" in reference to the decision. But Ali knew he had lost fairly. "Shut up," said Ali. "Nobody got robbed. I lost the fight."

"Shut up. Nobody got robbed. I lost the fight."

—Ali

After the fight, Ali departed for a tour of the Soviet Union. He boxed two exhibitions and met with Soviet leader Leonid Brezhnev. Spinks was enjoying his new-found celebrity, but the trappings of success quickly caught up with the young champion. Shortly after the bout, he was arrested for cocaine possession, and a progression of legal problems—some minor, some not—would plague him for the remainder of his pro career.

"Leon was training in Philadelphia at that time of his career, so he was one of the guys I'd see in the gym," said Collins. "He was always being compared to Michael. It was always, 'How come he can't be more like his brother? How come he doesn't have Michael's personality?' I just thought of Leon as another wild and crazy fighter who didn't know how to handle his fame. At that point, it was hard to feel sorry for him. He was making millions of dollars and obviously enjoying himself."

Comparisons to Michael were inevitable. Michael Spinks was more articulate and a better fighter. In

1983, Michael became the undisputed light-heavy-weight king, and in 1985 he became the first 175-pound champ in history to move up and capture the heavyweight crown. He and Leon remain the only brothers to have captured the heavyweight title. Michael achieved all of his success without the controversy and problems that haunted Leon. In 1994, Michael was inducted into the International Boxing Hall of Fame. The highlight of Leon's career, however, remains that first Ali fight.

In addition to Leon's legal troubles, the politics of boxing were also closing in on him in early 1978. The WBC threatened to strip him of the title if he did not make his first defense against Ken Norton. Working diligently behind the scenes was promoter Don King. King controlled much of the heavyweight division, with the notable exceptions of Spinks and Ali. In all likelihood, it was King's cozy relationship with WBC President Jose Suliaman that expedited the stripping of Spinks. On March 29, 1978, the WBC announced it would strip Spinks and name Norton the champion. In Norton's first title defense, he lost the crown to Larry Holmes, who was promoted by King.

The decision not to fight Norton seemed relatively easy for Spinks. He would earn a much larger purse for a rematch with Ali, and the WBA would still sanction it as a heavyweight championship fight. Thus, the rematch was scheduled for September 15, 1978, at the Superdome in New Orleans.

The Superdome was packed with 63,532 fans, an indoor attendance record for a boxing match. A live gate of $4,806,675 was generated, which was another record. It topped the $2,658,660 produced by the second Jack Dempsey-Gene Tunney fight in 1927.

Ali made sure he was ready for the September 1978 rematch with Spinks, which he won easily.

Ali's strategy for the rematch was simple. He would utilize his jab and keep the fight in the center of the ring. He would not resort to the Rope-a-Dope; rather, if he needed a rest, he would simply tie Spinks up in a clinch.

Spinks seemed to be without a strategy. Twice he vanished from training camp for the rematch, and his partying binges continued right up until the fight. He must have been convinced that he would again out-hustle his aging opponent.

Ali, in fantastic shape, weighed in at 221 pounds to Spinks's 201. Throughout the course of the fight, Leon plodded after Ali, absorbing jabs and right hands on the way in. Spinks's corner was also in disarray.

With too many voices chirping at the fighter, Benton left the corner after the sixth round.

Ultimately, no one could have saved Spinks from himself. He was out of shape, and the mental determination that had lifted him in the first fight was gone. Ali won a unanimous decision. The scoring by rounds was 10–4–1 (twice) and 11–4.

"The second fight was terrible compared to the first one," said Collins. "Ali won, but he really didn't do much. If it hadn't been the great Ali in the ring, the fight would have been panned as a lousy fight."

Nonetheless, at 36 years old, Ali had become the first man in the history of boxing to win the heavyweight title three times.

Once again, Ali claimed this would be his last fight. In Tom Hauser's biography, the champ is quoted as saying, "I'd be the biggest fool in the world to go out a loser after being the first three-time champ. None of the black athletes before me ever got out when they were on top. My people need one black man to come out on top. I've got to be the first."

On June 26, 1979, Ali officially announced his retirement from boxing. Fifteen months later, he would return to the ring.

The Roar of the Crowd

Ali was lured to the ring twice in the 1980s. The aging champ fought for money and adulation, but it was painfully obvious that he had little left.

Boxing history is littered with the broken bodies of fighters who fought on when they should have retired. A sad byproduct of the sport is witnessing a faded warrior—deceived by his own sense of invincibility—conclude a noble career with a humiliating defeat at the hands of a younger, stronger champion.

Muhammad Ali never seemed destined for that kind of finish. He was too smart, too ambitious, and too vain to sacrifice his reputation and body for one last payday, one last moment in the spotlight. In Thomas Hauser's book *Muhammad Ali: His Life and Times*, Hall of Famer Archie Moore, who fought until the age of 49, recalled a day in 1960 when Ali told him he would not have a long boxing career. "I don't want to fight to be an old man," Ali told Moore. "That's all right for you, but I'm gonna only fight five or six years, make me two or three million dollars, and quit fighting."

But like those before him, and even those who came after him, Ali could not free himself from the grip boxing had upon his spirit.

Shortly after he defeated Leon Spinks and regained the heavyweight title, Ali announced his retirement from the ring. It should have been a fitting ending. The self-proclaimed "greatest of all time" made a strong case for himself by winning the heavyweight crown an unprecedented third time. Ali retired confident of his standing in boxing history.

Yet after two years of inactivity, Ali was persuaded into taking on a new challenge. The sad lessons witnessed at the close of the careers of John L. Sullivan, Joe Louis, and Sugar Ray Robinson were suddenly lost on Ali. As an aging champion, the lure of the spotlight and an $8 million purse were too strong.

The new challenge was in the form of Larry Holmes, Ali's former sparring partner, who had assumed the throne of king of the heavyweights.

As Ali proceeded with his comeback, signs suggesting that it was ill advised were beginning to manifest. His longtime friend and photographer, Howard Bingham, was against the fight. Dr. Ferdie Pacheco, who dropped out of Ali's corner after the Earnie Shavers fight because he felt Ali should have retired then, was also critical of Ali's decision to fight.

Questions were also raised about the 38-year-old Ali's health leading up to the match. Before the Nevada State Athletic Commission would sanction the contest, they made Ali undergo a battery of tests at the Mayo

Ali, with his daughter MayMay at New York City's Hard Rock Cafe in May 1981. He donated the robe given to him by Elvis Presley to the eatery.

Clinic in Minnesota. While the Mayo Clinic ultimately gave Ali a clean bill of health, there were comments in the report filed with the athletic commission that should have raised some flags. The findings, published in the neurological report and in Hauser's book, read in part: "...he does not quite hop with the agility that one might anticipate and on finger to nose testing there is a slight degree of missing the target. Both of these tests could be significantly influenced by fatigue."

Ali did say that he was tired on the day of the evaluation, but should a world-class athlete who is about to challenge for the heavyweight title have problems with those simple tests? Despite the report, the officials in Nevada gave Ali's comeback a green light.

In his book *Muhammad Ali: A View from the Corner*, Pacheco argues that the best people to judge whether a fighter is capable of fighting are the trainers who hang out in the boxing gyms every day. "Doctors who see a fighter once, on the day of the fight, cannot begin to compare with [trainers] as judges of the deterioration of a fighter," wrote Pacheco. "A fighter who is in excellent health, by routine physical examination, can still be a shot fighter in the ring."

Ultimately, Ali listened only to one voice, and that was his own. "Where else can I make that kind of money in an hour?" Ali rationalized. While Holmes held the title, Ali held the public's imagination and therefore took the lion's share of the purse. He was guaranteed $8 million while Holmes was to receive $2.3 million.

Holmes served as Ali's sparring partner from 1973 to 1975. When he was a child, Holmes idolized the champion, and as he grew older he respected and admired Ali. By '75, Holmes began appearing on Ali's undercards. He had knocked out Rodney Bobick on the undercard of the "Thrilla in Manila" and had decisioned Roy Williams on the same night that Ali defeated Jimmy Young. In 1978, Holmes captured the WBC heavyweight title with a grueling 15-round decision over Ken Norton. He had made seven successful title defenses—all by knockout—when he signed to meet Ali in 1980. Among his more notable victims were Mike Weaver and Shavers.

The fight was not one the Holmes camp wanted, but promoter Don King insisted on putting it together. Ali, despite his age, was still boxing's biggest draw. Holmes was uncomfortable with the idea that he might have to humiliate his hero. But the business of boxing necessitated it.

"It was a no-win fight for us," said Richie Giachetti, Holmes's trainer. "I was against it. If Ali managed to look good, the media would have criticized us. If we knocked him out, then everybody would have said, 'Well, you just beat an old man.'"

Nonetheless, the fight was made, and once the promotion was in full swing, Ali found himself back in his element. He was back on center stage and back in front of the TV cameras. That kind of power and popularity can be intoxicating. He quickly nicknamed Holmes "The Peanut" because, he said, that's how his head was shaped, and he promised to "shell" him during the fight. Drumming up further interest in the contest, Ali said, "He's no Liston. He's no Foreman. He's no Frazier. He's only Larry Holmes, and he's nothing. He's just the man between me and my fourth title."

Although Holmes was a month shy of his 31st birthday and a champion at the peak of his career, he entered the ring only a slight favorite. The reason was the weigh-in. Holmes weighed in at 211 pounds and Ali weighed 217, the lightest he'd been since facing George Foreman. When the betting crowd saw Ali's fantastic physical appearance, they drove the odds down from 3-to-1 for Holmes to 13-to-10 in favor of Ali.

"It was unbelievable," recalled Giachetti. "These were so-called boxing experts in the media picking Ali to win. But Ali had slipped. Larry had no fear of him because they had sparred so much. I saw Larry spar 1,000 rounds with Ali. And Larry got the better of him. Things weren't going to be different in a real fight."

Steve Farhood, a boxing writer and broadcaster who at the time was the editor-in-chief of *KO Magazine*, recalled how easy it was to be swayed by the great Ali. "Given what we all knew, I remember thinking that the odds were absurd," he said. "But I wouldn't bet the fight. I think the Ali mystique was so great that you kind of expected some magic. With Ali, it was easy to suspend the truth. Then after three rounds, you realized there was no magic."

The bout took place on October 2, 1980, at Caesar's Palace in Las Vegas. The 24,740 fans in attendance generated a record live gate of $5,766,125. Ali was listless, offering little in return against Holmes's

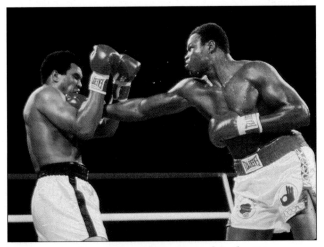

Holmes, in the prime of his career, hit the 38-year-old Ali at will.

swift salvos. Holmes punished him for 10 ugly rounds before Angelo Dundee stopped the fight with Ali sitting on his stool. Ali never went down but was battered repeatedly by Holmes. At various times throughout the one-sided contest, Holmes looked at the referee, hoping he would intervene and stop the fight.

"It was pathetic to watch," said Farhood. "You knew the only reason Holmes was hitting Ali was because he had to. And the only reason Ali was still there was because he had a tremendous heart."

After the fight, Ali spent two days at the UCLA Medical Center. It was revealed that Ali was taking medication that was improperly prescribed by Dr. Charles

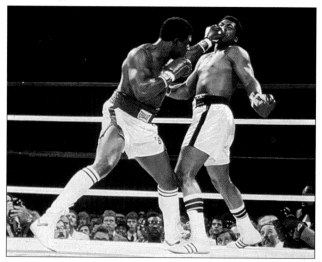

It was evident to all that Ali had nothing left when he fought Trevor Berbick in his final fight in December 1981.

Williams, the personal physician of Elijah Muhammad. Williams had told Ali that he was suffering from a hypothyroid condition and gave him a drug called Thyrolar. While the use of that drug helped Ali lose weight, it unfortunately left him fatigued and dehydrated before the fight. It was a mistake that could have cost Ali his life. Unfortunately, it would provide him with another excuse to return to the ring.

To the athlete, adulation is a drug that can be more powerful than any banned substance. Some fighters come back for the money. Others come back just to hear the crowd chant their name one more time. Ali came back for both.

"He has the same problem that many celebrities have: He was addicted to the attention," said Nikos Spanakos, who was Ali's teammate on the 1960 Olympic team and today is a professor. "After he'd speak at my school, he would whisper in my ear, 'Take me to where there is a crowd of people.' He always wanted to perform. He needed that adulation. That's probably why he boxed for so long."

The embarrassment of the Holmes fight did not deter Ali from returning to the ring. He blamed his poor performance on the medication. He managed to convince himself and those around him that a drug, not Larry Holmes, defeated Ali. The rationale for fighting again was that a healthy Ali could defeat a fringe contender like Trevor Berbick.

"I wasn't surprised that he came back," said Farhood. "After the Holmes fight, you kind of had the feeling he wanted to go out better. I learned quickly that retirement is not a word you take literally in boxing."

At this point, the Ali mystique had faded so much that the promoter could not find a site in the United

States. The fight wound up taking place in a minor-league baseball stadium in the Bahamas on December 11, 1981. The promotion was in disarray up until the night of the fight. The gates to the stadium were still locked at fight time, forcing many spectators and journalists to climb a fence into the ballpark. There were only two pairs of gloves for all the undercard fighters, and no one had thought to bring a bell.

"Father Time caught up with me. I'm finished."
—Ali

Berbick, a fighter who had moderate skills but a stubborn streak, had a 20–2–1 record when he met Ali. Eight months earlier, he had lost a bid to win the title from Holmes. Berbick, though, would go on to win the WBC heavyweight crown in 1986, during a time when the division was mired in mediocrity.

Like Holmes, he entered the ring against Ali with a feeling of ambivalence.

"It was a great motivation to fight him," said Berbick. "But then there was a sympathy. I'm saying, how can I ever really, really hurt him, try to really hurt him seriously? I was hoping that I'd hit him and he'd just go down and out instead of banging at him hard.

"I knew I had to do what I had to do. So I stayed with the body because I figured it would do less damage. And I scored a lot to the body. Even when he was on me, I was punching tremendously. That's what won me the fight."

The fight was dull, and it was immediately clear that Ali had nothing left. Berbick was the aggressor, but he lacked the skills to look impressive against an over-the-hill champion. In the end, Berbick was awarded a 10-round unanimous decision.

"The fight was uneventful," recalled Farhood. "But there are things about that night I'll never forget. Someone sang 'America the Beautiful' as Ali walked to the ring. I watched half of it live and half of it on a monitor in front of me. Watching him walk to the ring was very emotional. This was history to me. I realized at that moment that I'd probably never see another fighter like that again. It was special."

At the postfight press conference, Ali announced his retirement. "Father Time caught up with me," he said. "I'm finished."

Ed Schuyler, the longtime boxing writer for the Associated Press, expressed the gracious yet somber emotions of the boxing media when he said, "Muhammad, thank you. You gave us a hell of a ride."

The Legend Lives On

Ali now suffers from Parkinson's syndrome, a nonfatal neurological disease. His mind is still sharp and he travels extensively, inspiring people throughout the world.

T he hands that once flashed across the boxing ring in a blur now quiver. The voice that shouted "I shocked the world" and "I am the greatest" has been muted to a whisper. Muhammad Ali, whose popularity and charisma reached global proportions throughout his brilliant boxing career, has been slowed by an illness that resulted primarily from that career.

Today, the image of Ali, sedate in almost a trance-like state, is a troublesome sight for many of those who witnessed him in his athletic splendor. Muhammad, now 57 years old, suffers from Parkinson's syndrome. It is a nonfatal neurological disorder that has developed from his extended career in the ring. The characteristics that Ali displays—tremors, poor balance, and difficulty speaking—are all byproducts of Parkinson's syndrome.

"It's very, very sad to see him today," said Steve Acunto, cofounder of the American Association for the Improvement of Boxing and a member of the New York State Athletic Commission for over 50 years. "What makes it even harder to accept is that it probably shouldn't have happened. Muhammad could have walked away from boxing, but he didn't. I'd imagine with all the adulation that still surrounds him, it makes him feel good. He deserves that. He's a great humanitarian."

Parkinson's syndrome does afflict many non-boxers. It is usually found in people over the age of 60, or it can develop in younger people after acute encephalitis, carbon monoxide poisoning, or repeated physical trauma. In the case of Ali, that physical trauma was repeated blows to the head that destroyed cells in the brain stem. Those cells are supposed to produce the neurotransmitter dopamine, which controls voluntary movement.

Ali was first diagnosed with this illness in 1984. While his symptoms affect his motor skills, speech, and facial expressions, Parkinson's syndrome has not incapacitated him intellectually. His mind remains sharp. His thought process has been unaffected and his memory is very good.

The biggest misconception about Ali's health is the severity of his illness. While his symptoms worsen when he is fatigued or when he is not taking the proper dosages of his medication, his health is not as bad as it appears. In Thomas Hauser's biography, *Muhammad Ali: His Life and Times,* he reported that, aside from the Parkinson's, Ali's general health was good.

Another important fact about Ali's health is that he does not suffer from pugilistica dementia, the medical term for being punch drunk.

"His physical appearance may be one thing, but there doesn't appear to be a mental breakdown," said Acunto. "His wit is still pretty sharp."

Despite his outward appearance, Ali still maintains a high energy level. He spends as many as 200 days per year on the road. He earns a substantial income by making public appearances and by attending autograph and sports memorabilia shows. Due to his widespread popularity, his travels often take him to foreign countries. In 1986, Ali married his fourth wife, Lonnie. She often accompanies him on the road and helps handle his business affairs.

"Muhammad's travel schedule would be taxing for someone who is half his age," said Harlan Werner, president of Sports Placement Services, the company that represents Ali in the sports memorabilia market. "Muhammad is in tremendous demand."

In November 1990, Ali made what was called a "nonpolitical...humanitarian mission" visit to Iraq. While the United States was on the verge of war with Iraq, Ali met with President Saddam Hussein and urged that he find a peaceful solution to the conflict. While the Gulf War began two months later, Ali's visit with Hussein resulted in the release of American hostages that were taken when Iraq invaded Kuwait in August 1990.

While Ali has never disappeared from the world stage, he has enjoyed a resurgence since lighting the torch at the 1996 Summer Olympic Games in Atlanta. His surprise appearance was one of the most dramatic moments in Olympic history. To the tune of "Ode to

Although Parkinson's syndrome has affected his speech, Ali travels regularly. In 1993, he went to Iraq to gain the release of political prisoners.

Joy" from Beethoven's Ninth, former Olympian and world heavyweight champion Evander Holyfield passed the torch to gold-medal swimmer Janet Evans. As Evans ascended the ramp to the torch, Ali appeared at its apex. Muhammad, his hands shaking, then lit the torch to officially start the Games.

A few nights later, Ali managed to upstage the USA basketball "Dream Team" when he was presented with a gold medal to replace the one he won in 1960. Ali had thrown his 1960 Olympic gold medal into a river to protest racism in America. International Olympic

A worldwide television audience cheered as the world's most famous athlete lit the Olympic flame at the 1996 Atlanta Games.

Committee President Juan Antonio Samaranch made the presentation at midcourt of the Georgia Dome as a record men's Olympic basketball crowd of 34,600 cheered in approval of the gesture and the champion.

Then, in 1997, came the release of *When We Were Kings*, a documentary about Ali's fight with George Foreman in Zaire. The film won an Academy Award, and Ali and Foreman accompanied director Leon Gast to the stage on Oscar night.

Yet as touching as those moments were—the Olympics and the Oscars—the image that sticks with most people is the physical condition of Ali.

"People shouldn't feel sad for Muhammad," said Tom Loeffler, a boxing manager who represents fighters under the banner of Mouthpiece Productions, which is a sister company of Sports Placement Services. "As far as his life, he's very happy. He's one of the most fulfilled people I've ever met. It makes him feel bad when people feel sorry for him."

In recent years, Ali has also refined his religious beliefs. He has converted to Orthodox Islam, which is practiced widely around the world. He is no longer associated with the Nation of Islam and that sect's divisive teachings. A devout Muslim, Ali prays five times a day and regularly reads the Koran.

Ali has also appeared before Congress to help lobby for research money for Parkinson's and other diseases. Senator John McCain (Republican from Arizona), who led a Senate subcommittee investigating boxing, proposed the Muhammad Ali Boxing Reform Act, which would curb "exploitative and coercive" practices by promoters. Thanks to the efforts of McCain, the Professional Boxing Safety Act became law in 1996.

Another effort Ali has recently dedicated himself to is a campaign against bigotry and hatred. He's collaborated with Hauser on a book called *Healing: A Journal of Tolerance and Understanding*. In it, Ali says, "I wish people would love everybody else the way they love me. It would be a better world."

There remains no shortage of love for Muhammad Ali. His presence generates an electricity that crosses racial, religious, and social boundaries. He is indeed still the people's champion.

"When he walks into a room, the aura that he has will command the attention of everyone in that room," said Loeffler. "I've never seen anything like that. His

Ali and George Foreman get together at the 1997 Academy Awards, where the documentary about their fight, When We Were Kings, *won an Oscar.*

impact reaches everyone. It's ironic in that now he doesn't speak as much or as loudly, but he has become a more powerful presence. He dictates attention by his actions."

When Ali is introduced at a boxing event, he receives the largest ovation. When he is around other fighters, some of them great champions in their own right, those men drown in the wake of fans trying to get close to Ali. In boxing, there is Ali and then there is everyone else. After one such event, his longtime friend and photographer, Howard Bingham, was asked if the enthusiasm over Ali will ever wane.

"This is how it's been all day, every day for 30 years," said Bingham. "Ali has no end."

CHAPTER 16

Ali's Legacy

Experts are divided on whether Ali is the greatest heavyweight of all time. One thing is clear, however: No athlete in history has ever made a greater impact on the world.

A s the 20th century draws to a close, it seems like the appropriate time to put Muhammad Ali in historical perspective. Perhaps more than with any other athlete, the Ali mystique has extended to all corners of the globe. He can be recalled many different ways: as Olympic hero, heavyweight king, champion of the underprivileged, conscientious objector, and goodwill ambassador.

"When you look at today's athletes, so few of them represent anything," said Leon Carter, deputy sports editor of the New York *Daily News*. "They take a stand on whether or not they are getting enough endorsements. My African-American heroes, in no particular order, are Jackie Robinson, Arthur Ashe, and Muhammad Ali. Those are my top three. I would not put

Michael Jordan in that lot. It's reserved for people who stood for something."

Before Ali touched the masses, he needed a stage on which to perform. That stage was boxing. Most historians generally agree that the two greatest heavyweight champions in history are Ali and Joe Louis. The arguments for each are compelling. Louis was a boxer/puncher equipped with devastating power. He held the heavyweight title from 1937 until 1949 and made a record 25 title defenses. Ali was the first three-time heavyweight champion and the most graceful boxer of his era. The largest factor in distinguishing Ali from Louis is the caliber of competition. Ali fought during the 1970s, a decade of great heavyweights. While Louis's longevity is impressive, and he certainly dominated his era, his opponents did not measure up to Ali's.

When selecting Ali or Louis, boxing experts are clearly divided by generation. Consider these thoughts from those who covered Ali, fought him, worked with him, or worked against him:

George Chuvalo, who fought Ali in 1966 and 1972: "I think when Ali was at his best, he would have beaten any heavyweight champ in history. People talk about Joe Louis. Well, Louis had trouble with Billy Conn, who was a smaller version of Ali. It's easy for me to say this because it was my era, but I really believe that Ali fought in the best heavyweight era in history. And Ali didn't turn his back on too many opponents. You just had to get in line."

Bill Gallo, a columnist and cartoonist for the New York *Daily News* who has covered boxing for more than 40 years: "The greatest heavyweight champion I ever saw was Joe Louis. I would put Ali third after

In 1976, Ali sat with former champs (left to right) *Floyd Patterson, Jack Dempsey, Joe Louis, Joe Frazier, and Joe Walcott.*

Rocky Marciano. When I saw Louis, I saw a perfect fighter. He had a jab, he threw combinations, and he was a harder hitter than Ali. Ali was a great fighter. But in his prime, Louis was more of a complete fighter."

Eddie Futch, the Hall of Fame trainer who sparred with Louis and prepared two men to defeat Ali: "I think Louis was the best heavyweight champion in history. Ali is second. Louis would have had a tough time with Ali's speed and boxing ability. Billy Conn demonstrated that. Conn was one of the most skillful boxers of his day. But Louis would eventually catch up with Ali like he did with Conn. Louis boxed Primo Carnera, Abe Simon, and Buddy Baer, so size didn't matter as much. Louis had lightning-quick hands, and all his punches were thrown correctly."

The Statue of Liberty-Ellis Island Foundation honored Ali and baseball legend Joe DiMaggio for contributions to America.

Chuck Wepner, who challenged Ali in 1975: "I'd have to put Ali right near the top of the list. Ali, Louis, and Marciano are the three best heavyweights in history. In his prime, with his speed and power, Ali was tough to beat. He faced a lot of good heavyweights. When Rocky was champ, there weren't as many good heavyweights. And Louis had his "Bum of the Month Club.""

Steve Farhood, boxing writer and broadcaster: "To me, Ali and Louis are 1 and 1A. The difference is that Ali was blessed to fight in the best era in the history of the division. And look what he did in that era. When Ali was in his prime, when he was a champion, he was never really in a close fight. No one extended him. Ali's first reign was like Sugar Ray Robinson's as a welterweight. His second reign was like when Robinson was a middleweight. And he needed both to solidify his greatness."

Dr. Ferdie Pacheco, a boxing commentator who served as Ali's personal physician: "Ali had the guts of Jake LaMotta. He was as tough as he was pretty, and that's saying a lot. That's why I think he's the greatest fighter ever."

If Ali was indeed the greatest heavyweight in history, was he also the most important athlete in history? One men's magazine, GQ, has already proclaimed him "The Athlete of the Century." Babe Ruth and Jack Dempsey were the first exalted American sports figures. Pelé was the most popular participant in the world's most popular sport, soccer. In measuring their significance against Ali's in the narrow scope of sports, it is difficult to reach a conclusion. But Ali's impact extended well beyond the sports world. He was a social lightning rod in addition to being an outstanding athlete. In the turbulent 1960s, he came to symbolize numerous young Americans—black and white—who were struggling with their conscience and the authorities that governed the land.

"His fans and detractors were a barometer for the political winds of the time," said Greg Long, an editor in *Newsday*'s sports department who was of draft age in 1969. "I am a product of my times, true, but what other athlete had such an impact on his times? His story serves to enrich all Americans."

The way the world viewed Ali was shaped by those who covered him in the media. Throughout his professional life, Ali evolved from brash prodigy to hero of the counterculture to sentimental champion to revered icon. In the process, he redefined the relationship between the athlete and the media. Gallo and Dave Anderson, of *The New York Times,* witnessed the Ali roller coaster from beginning to end.

"The thinking of the world was different in the '60s," said Anderson. "You can't ask people to write or think in a different time period. People disliked him for a variety of reasons. The racists hated him because he was black. Religious people hated him because he was a Muslim. And a lot of people disliked him just because he was a braggart. Then you had the Army thing on top of it.

"But [the media] grew to love him. He was always available. Early on, he was more confrontational, but he was available. Some of the Muslims would say, 'You can't talk to him.' But then Ali would say, 'Yes, you can.' He was the best when it came to dealing with the media. He made it fun. The fighters before him were quiet guys. With Ali, there was this great breath of fresh air."

Gallo's view of Ali changed during the Vietnam War. "It took us a while to get used to him," he said. "At first, he came off as a loudmouth, a wiseguy. Then we realized he was putting us on—that he was laughing throughout everything he did. He was a tremendous promoter."

The legacy of Ali is on display in boxing rings around the world. Like young artists trying to emulate the strokes of Picasso, countless fighters have attempted to duplicate Ali's style, grace, and charisma.

"In 1979, I got picked to fight for the Muhammad Ali boxing team," said former two-time welterweight champion Mark Breland. "When I got off the bus, Ali came right over to me and started shadowboxing with me. He still remembers me to this day. I saw him in New York a few years ago and he waved me over. I felt like a little kid all over again. Ali is the one who got me into boxing. Everyone wanted to be like Ali.

"When I was starting out, I never saw the Ali shuffle. But I was doing it, or at least what I thought it was. We all tried to copy Ali in some way. Ali brought

Ali takes one on the chin from basketball legend Magic Johnson at a 1997 banquet in New York.

something different to boxing. Excitement. Charisma. You'll never find another Muhammad Ali again."

Ultimately, the essence of Ali, what lasts longer in our minds than the great fights, is his personality. He is most comfortable when he is around people, and his genuine warmth and love often rubs off on those near him.

"For personality and charisma, no one can hold a candle to Ali," said Richie Giachetti, who has trained Mike Tyson and Larry Holmes. "He treated me with nothing but class, and there were times when I was the only white guy up at his Deer Lake training camp. He's one of the nicest guys I've ever met. He's the icon of icons. He's a great human being."

Ali has brought a smile to millions of faces. He has touched the hearts of the rich, the poor, the young, the old, and people of all colors. Never in our history has there been an athlete who has meant so much to so many.